THE NEW MERMAIDS

The Beaux' Stratagem

THE NEW MERMAIDS

General Editor
BRIAN GIBBONS
Professor of English Literature, University of Zürich

Previous general editors have been
PHILIP BROCKBANK
BRIAN MORRIS
ROMA GILL

The Beaux' Stratagem

GEORGE FARQUHAR

Edited by
MICHAEL CORDNER
Lecturer in English, University of York

LONDON/A & C BLACK

NEW YORK/W W NORTON

Fourth impression 1990
Published by A & C Black (Publishers) Limited
35 Bedford Row, London WC1R 4JH

First published in this form 1976
by Ernest Benn Limited

Published in the United States of America by
W. W. Norton and Company, Inc.
500 Fifth Avenue, New York, N.Y. 10110

ISBN 0–7136–3042–6
ISBN 0–393–90007–X (USA)

Printed in Great Britain by
Richard Clay Ltd, Bungay, Suffolk

CONTENTS

ACKNOWLEDGEMENTS

IN PREPARING THE ANNOTATIONS for this edition, I have made full use of the labours of previous editors—in particular, H. Macauley Fitzgibbon (1898), Louis A. Strauss (1914), Charles Stonehill (1930), Henry Nettleton and A. E. Case (1939), Vincent F. Hopper and Gerald B. Lahey (1963), Eric Rothstein (1967), and A. Norman Jeffares (1972). Where excerpts from these editions are cited in the notes of the present volume, the quotation is accompanied by the relevant editor's surname.

I would like to thank the Librarian of Cambridge University Library for permission to reproduce the title-page of that library's copy of the first quarto of *The Beaux' Stratagem.*

I am very pleased to be able to record my gratitude for the help provided during the editing of the play by Marie and Richard Axton, Ron Clayton, Eva and Tony Fox, and Nick Havely. Thanks are similarly due to Brian Gibbons for the care with which he scrutinized the completed text. I also owe long-standing debts to two people with whom I have enjoyed many lengthy and indispensable conversations on seventeenth- and eighteenth-century drama—Anne Barton and Norman Stevenson.

University of York   MICHAEL CORDNER
December 1974

INTRODUCTION

THE AUTHOR

GEORGE FARQUHAR WAS BORN IN LONDONDERRY, in the North of Ireland, in 1677 or 1678.[1] His father was a penurious clergyman of the Church of England who was confronted with the unenviable task of rearing seven children on a stipend of £150 a year. The clergyman was also a victim of the violent aftermath in Ireland of the Glorious Revolution of 1688; he is said to have been burned out of his home by Catholic supporters of James II and to have died shortly thereafter.

The future dramatist entered Trinity College, Dublin, as a sizar in 1694. The position of a sizar was a rather humiliating one, since these students supported themselves at university by small allowances which they received in return for the performance of such menial duties as waiting at table. In 1695, Farquhar managed to escape from this servile drudgery by winning an exhibition worth £4, but, within a very short time, he became embroiled in a row at Donnybrook Fair and was disciplined by being suspended from his exhibition (he was reinstated early the next year).[2]

He left Trinity in 1696 and took up an acting career with the company of the Smock Alley playhouse in Dublin. Eighteenth-century comments on his acting abilities tend to be affectionate but scarcely enthusiastic. In any case, his acting career was abruptly terminated (probably in early 1697) by an accident during a performance of Dryden's *The Indian Emperor*. Farquhar, forgetting to use a blunted sword, 'wounded the Person that represented *Vasquez*, tho' (as it fell out) not dangerously'.[3] He was, however, too badly shaken by the event to continue with an acting career.

He proceeded to London—possibly on the advice of Robert Wilks, who was a member of the Smock Alley company at the time,

[1] The contemporary materials on Farquhar's life are quite copious and have been neatly drawn together by Eric Rothstein, *George Farquhar* (New York, 1967), pp. 13–29. Unless otherwise specified, documentation for the assertions made in the following biographical sketch will be found in Rothstein's chapter.

[2] Peter Kavanagh, 'George Farquhar', *The Times Literary Supplement*, 10 February 1945, p. 72.

[3] W. R. Chetwood, *A General History Of The Stage* (London, 1749), pp. 149–50.

and whose considerable talents were soon to be displayed in the London performances of Farquhar's comedies. In 1698, the first of these, *Love and a Bottle*, received its première in London (though without Wilks in the cast) and achieved a moderate success. In the same year, an anonymous prose work (now usually attributed to Farquhar), *The Adventures of Covent Garden*, appeared in print. But it was in November 1699 that his first major success was unveiled to the playgoing public—the comedy *The Constant Couple, or A Trip to the Jubilee*. This was one of the most immediately and most splendidly successful plays of the entire period. However, it was disappointingly succeeded by three comedies which failed almost totally to win the approval of contemporary audiences—*Sir Harry Wildair* (1701), *The Inconstant* (1702), and *The Twin-Rivals* (1702). In these same years, Farquhar wrote, in addition, quite a substantial amount of fairly ephemeral non-dramatic prose and verse.

The slump in his fortunes as a writer coincided unhappily with a fairly drastic crisis in his personal life. Farquhar married Margaret Pemell, a widow with two children, under the mistaken conviction (which the lady had deceitfully encouraged) that she was the possessor of a proud fortune; in fact, she was quite penniless. Eighteenth-century biographers inform us that, against all the odds, the marriage, in time, became an affectionate and relatively stable one, but the immediate result was obviously an alarming worsening in his financial situation. Several writers have not unreasonably suggested a connection between Farquhar's unfortunate marriage and the dramatist's preoccupation, in his final comedy, with Milton's treatise on divorce. In the absence of any testimony from early biographers on this subject, however, it seems best to tread very carefully here.

One immediate response to these new exigencies was the writing of a short farce, *The Stage-Coach*. This proved a thoroughly popular afterpiece, though it is unlikely that, in the event, Farquhar made very much money from it. A second response was his securing a lieutenancy (in 1704) in the earl of Orrery's Regiment of Foot. No solution to his money problems was, however, to be found in this new calling; indeed, it appears that Farquhar was actually financially disadvantaged by his energetic efforts to recruit soldiers for the regiment.[4] But from these latter experiences came the materials which form the basis of one of his two finest comedies, *The Recruiting Officer*. First performed in April 1706, it was overwhelmingly successful and restored a measure of health to its creator's finances.

There is some doubt about the next steps in his career, but it

[4] Robert John Jordan, 'George Farquhar's Military Career', *Huntington Library Quarterly*, vol. 37 (1973-74), 251-64.

appears likely that he proceeded to resign his lieutenancy on the basis of a promise (made by the duke of Ormonde) that the latter would secure him a captaincy—a promise which remained conspicuously unfulfilled.[5] So, once again, financial catastrophe struck, and *The Beaux' Stratagem*, his last comedy, was written in circumstances of the greatest need. By now, Farquhar was gravely ill, and he did not live long after the first performance of his masterpiece on 8 March 1707. He was buried on 23 May.

THE PLAY

The Beaux' Stratagem, Farquhar's final comedy, was an immediate and lasting success with eighteenth-century audiences. It became a regular item in the playhouse repertoire and one of that select group of extremely popular plays which tended to be singled out for early performance in most seasons. The logic behind this was that, since the actors could be relied upon to be already fairly familiar with these plays, very little rehearsal would be required and the time saved could be used in preparing new or less familiar works.[6] Another indication of the play's widespread appeal is the rather remarkable fame which some of its more striking characters rapidly earned for themselves. Lady Bountiful, of course, graciously bequeathed her name to the English language; the same is true of Boniface, whose name became, as a result of the play, a generic title for an innkeeper. This latter character appears to have had a particular attraction for contemporary audiences. Within a month of the play's first appearance, a performance could be advertised as being 'For the benefit of Will Bullock, as the saying is'; the innkeeper's characteristic ejaculation had obviously become a popular catchphrase. In time, the play even gained the spurious subtitle 'The Litchfield Landlord'.[7] Similarly, Norris, who played Squire Sullen's servant, was made to identify himself jokingly as Scrub, while performing the prologue of a Vanbrugh play in 1709; clearly the confident expectation was that the audience would, without any further prompting, be able to identify what character, and what play, were being referred to.[8]

[5] ibid., esp. 262–3.
[6] Emmett L. Avery (ed.), *The London Stage 1660–1800* Part 2: *1700–1729* (Carbondale, Illinois, 1960), pp. cxii–cxiii.
[7] ibid., p. 144; Sybil Rosenfeld, *Strolling Players and Drama in the Provinces 1660–1765* (Cambridge, 1939), pp. 225–47.
[8] Philip Roberts, 'Vanbrugh's Lost Play: The Prologue', *Restoration and Eighteenth-Century Theatre Research*, vol. 12 (1973), 57.

The particular potency of Farquhar's dramatic style was naturally a subject of much eighteenth-century debate. Writing probably in 1708, Benjamin Lintot, who had published *The Beaux' Stratagem*, was confident that he possessed the explanation. He detected in the writings of the dead Irishman a particular mastery in delineating 'the several Humours of his Time': 'he that in late Posterity would look for the Humours of this Age, must search Mr. *Farquhar* for them as much as he would *Vandike, Vario, Lilly*, or *Mr. Howard*, for their Personages or their Habits'. It was an answer that was echoed by others. In 1773, for example, William Woodfall praised 'Vanbrugh, Congreve, and Farquhar; the great merit of whose Comedies is, that they represent the manners of the times'.[9] This is a kind of praise which, on the evidence of his own critical writings, Farquhar would have found especially palatable. The whole argument of his *Discourse upon Comedy* (published in 1702) suggests that he would have emphatically agreed with John Dennis's declaration that a comic poet 'does nothing at all, if he does not draw the Pictures of his Contemporaries'.[10] Farquhar regards with astringent scepticism those who would judge modern writing for the stage by standards derived from the highest achievements of ancient Greece and ancient Rome. 'The rules of English comedy', he argues, 'do not lie in the compass of Aristotle or his followers, but in the pit, box, and galleries'. He stresses those factors of national and cultural difference too easily ignored by critical legislators obsessed with the application of classi-cally-derived formulae:

> An English play is intended for the use and instruction of an English audience, a people not only separated from the rest of the world by situation, but different also from other nations as well in the complexion and temperament of the natural body as in the constitution of our body politic.

Accordingly, those writing for contemporary London audiences need 'have nothing to do with the models of Menander or Plautus, but must consult Shakespeare, Jonson, Fletcher, and others, who by methods much different from the ancients have supported the English stage and made themselves famous to posterity'. But, as his prologue to *The Beaux' Stratagem* indicates, even here some cau-tion in the following of precedent was advisable. He praises Wycher-ley's *The Plain Dealer*, but as a comedy which 'lashed those crimes/

[9] *The Comedies of George Farquhar* (London, n.d.), To John Eyre, Esq; G. S. Rousseau (ed.), *Goldsmith: The Critical Heritage* (London, 1974), p.115.
[10] John Dennis, 'Remarks on a play, call'd, The Conscious Lovers, a comedy' (1723), *Critical Works*, ed. Edward Niles Hooker (Baltimore, 1943), vol. 2, 259.

Which then infested most'; one implication clearly is that a work of comparable stature written in 1707 would necessarily be radically different, since it would have to be preoccupied with what *now* 'infested most'. Another important variable had also to be taken into account. Farquhar is consistently clear-sighted about the radically diverse demands made upon the struggling and hopeful dramatist by different sections of his potentially cantankerous audience. 'The scholar calls upon us for decorums and economy; the courtier cries out for wit and purity of style; the citizen, for humor and ridicule; the divines threaten us for immodesty; and the ladies will have an intrigue'. Later in his treatise, he summarizes the playwright's task as a courageous attempt to satisfy simultaneously 'a pit full of Covent Garden gentlemen, a gallery full of cits, a hundred ladies of court education, and about two hundred footmen of nice morality'.[11] In the approximately democratic way in which he describes them, roughly equal importance is allotted to the demands of each faction in the audience. Even the footmen's point of view has to be carefully considered, as was merely prudent, since strong evidence exists of that group's willingness literally to cause a riot in the playhouse if dissatisfied with the entertainment offered.[12] The play's stage history during the eighteenth century firmly demonstrates Farquhar's ability to speak eloquently and satisfyingly to those who frequented the contemporary playhouses. In thinking about his comedy, it is worth bearing in mind, as he did, just how various were the attitudes and backgrounds of the members of his audience and, consequently, how adroit and resourceful any entertainment would have to be that aspired truly to please all of them.

The masterpieces of the Restoration comic tradition had been overwhelmingly urban and metropolitan in setting and outlook; Farquhar's last two comedies offered their audiences something decidedly different. The fairly automatic assumption had developed that, in contemporary comedy, country characters were fated to a largely unsympathetic and mocking treatment. Indeed, Farquhar recorded that, when it became known that *The Recruiting Officer* was set in Shrewsbury, his Shropshire friends became 'apprehensive that, by the example of some others, I would make the town merry at the expense of the country gentlemen'. He protested that

[11] The quotations from the *Discourse upon Comedy* are taken from Scott Elledge (ed.), *Eighteenth-Century Critical Essays* (Ithaca, New York, 1961), vol. 1, 93–4, 92, 94, 81, 82.
[12] Leo Hughes, *The Drama's Patrons: A Study of the Eighteenth-Century London Audience* (Austin and London, 1971), pp. 15 ff.

nothing could more have misrepresented his true intentions.[13] As was the case with Shrewsbury, Farquhar had visited Lichfield, the setting of *The Beaux' Stratagem*, in the course of his duties as a recruiting officer, and writers were later to offer unsubstantiated reports that characters in the play were based upon real people he had encountered during his time in Staffordshire.[14] Although these identifications are unreliable, such a search for non-fictitious sources for his characters does suggest a lively consciousness of the density and accuracy of Farquhar's portrait of the society of a small country town.[15] He does not, of course, ask us to forget London and all that it stood for in the life of the nation; indeed, the capital's influence is everywhere a potent factor in the development of the action. The crucial objective of the two beaux, for example, is to amass sufficient money to return for a further sampling of its delights, and the latter are very powerfully felt by Mrs Sullen and, as the play proceeds, by Dorinda (IV.i, 412 ff.). Gibbet hopes to end his life in respectable employment there (IV.ii, 145–6), and even Scrub is interested in discovering 'the newest flourish in whetting' knives, valuable information which can, of course, only be obtained from a servant freshly arrived from the metropolis (III.iii, 118–19).

The sixteenth and seventeenth centuries had witnessed an extraordinary growth in the economic power, political influence, and sheer size of London. By 1700 perhaps as many as one in ten of the population lived there; to understand the full significance of that figure, it needs to be compared with populations less than a tenth of that size in the next largest towns. It was thus merely natural that, in varying tones of excoriation and celebration, contemporaries should repeatedly discern a radical difference between the ways of life characteristic of the capital and those normal, indeed traditional, in the rest of the country. In particular, many voices testified that, in the relatively restless and experimental atmosphere of London, traditional notions of hierarchy and social order were frequently treated with less than the careful reverence they might be deemed to deserve. Thus, in a prose dialogue of 1693, an advocate of country ways can energetically argue that the greater stability of social relationships there constitutes one of the main advantages of his chosen dwelling-place. As he asserts, 'ev'ry one in the Country moves in his proper Sphere'. For example, 'the Yeomandry trudge on honestly in their several Vocations, without assuming the regulation of Things

---

[13] The Epistle Dedicatory to *The Recruiting Officer*.

[14] See, for example, Rev. Thomas Harwood, *The History and Antiquities of the Church and City of Lichfield* (Gloucester, 1806), p. 501.

[15] For an argument on these lines, see Rothstein, op. cit., pp. 143–4.

above their Capacity, as yours do in Town'.[16] Early in *The Beaux'*
Stratagem, Archer and Aimwell describe the life they have regretfully
left behind in London in terms which closely coincide with that
writer's analysis. They tell us how Jack Generous, a man of noble
extraction, is consigned to oblivion by his erstwhile friends once his
funds are exhausted; whereas Jack Handicraft, clearly of plebeian
origins, finds easy access to 'the best company in town' because his
talents for 'sharping' provide him with the necessary financial
qualification (I.i, 134). Any sense of people moving calmly and stably
in their proper spheres is obviously lacking in a social environment
where men of lowly and those of gentle birth exchange places in
the hierarchy for such reasons and with such brutal swiftness. Other
references to London ways in the play go further and develop a
contrast between them and the more conservative rhythms of life
elsewhere. For example, Mrs Sullen, anatomizing the unwelcome
restraints her marriage imposes upon her, sees in a return to London
the only satisfactory solution to her problems. There, the hallowed
authority of husband over wife, still an unpleasantly abiding reality
in Lichfield, will be triumphantly subverted by the contagiously rebellious traditions of the capital (II.i, 115 ff.). Our very first impres-
sions of the Lichfield townsfolk also work to develop the expectation
that a contrast of this kind will be sustained. Everything Boniface
says in his first conversation with the beaux exudes an atmosphere
of massive stability. He has 'lived in Lichfield, man and boy, above
eight and fifty years', and his evident pride in his 'good running
trade' and his tartly but discreetly independent attitude towards his
landlord and social superior, the squire, suggest a man surpassingly
comfortable and secure in his allotted role (I.i, 37, 98).

Yet Farquhar is not content to work with such a simple contrast
and moves swiftly to complicate it. In the course of that same opening scene, after all, we are to learn that this apparently respectable
innkeeper also serves as the industrious henchman of a gang of highwaymen, and he is destined to end the play fleeing from the law, his
respectability in tatters. Similar paradoxes can be traced in the histories of many of Lichfield's inhabitants. Boniface's daughter,
Cherry, whom we first see duly labouring as a servant in the inn,
claims to be impregnably convinced that her real father was the
possessor of nobler blood than a mere innkeeper's and accordingly
cultivates the habits of ladies of substantially higher rank than that

[16] [James Wright?], *The Humours and Conversations of the Town* (London,
1693), p. 103. For some fascinating comments on the effects of the growth of
London upon the seventeenth- and eighteenth-century imagination, see
E. A. Wrigley, 'London and the great leap forward', *The Listener*, 6 July
1967, pp. 7–8.

she currently endures. Foigard, whom everyone in Lichfield has accepted as a French priest (born in Brussels), is identified by the beaux as an Irish renegade, who, although indoctrinated by the masters of the impeccably Protestant school at Kilkenny, has deviated into allegiance to the Church of Rome. Gibbet, who earnestly aspires to be taken for a military gentleman (in spite of his spectacularly shabby uniform), is, in fact, a highwayman who robs in the hopes of achieving respectability by accumulating sufficient money to purchase himself a permanent position at court. Equally odd is the presence in the squire's household of a servant with the significant name of Gipsy, who 'dings about [the house] like a fury' (III.iii, 62). At the end of the play, she is sent off on her travels again, having been supplanted in her place by Cherry. Even the relatively unmoveable Scrub is permitted by his master no stability of calling but spends the week breathlessly moving through seven separate kinds of employment (III.iii, 88–92). Strikingly endemic among the members of this small rural community as Farquhar describes them is a quite bewildering and exhilarating mobility and ambiguity of social role and identity.

Presiding over this motley collection is the persistently inebriated Squire Sullen, who is, as Boniface tells us, 'a man of a great estate' who 'values nobody' (I.i, 85–6). But, while this gentleman's formidable material power is never questioned, there are characters who consider some of the more representative aspects of his behaviour deeply indecorous in a man of his rank. Such criticism is perhaps only to be expected from his much-abused wife and her sympathetic brother, but something more noteworthy is surely happening when even Gibbet is so appalled by the tawdriness of Sullen's boon companions, 'that, egad, I was ashamed to be seen in their company' (IV.ii, 127–28). Ironically, a not dissimilar accusation was levelled against Farquhar the dramatist by some eighteenth-century writers. Theophilus Cibber, for example, while finding much to admire in Farquhar's work, expressed some definite reservations: 'Had he lived to have gained a more general knowledge of life, or had his circumstances not been straitened, and so prevented his mingling with persons of rank, we might have seen his plays embellished with more finished characters, and with a more polish'd dialogue'.[17] A less tactfully phrased judgement upon Farquhar's handling of characters of rank was articulated by Horace Walpole, who remarked that 'Etherege, Congreve, Vanbrugh, and Cibber wrote genteel comedy, because they lived in the best company', whereas 'Farquhar's plays talk the language of a marching regiment in country quarters'—

[17] Theophilus Cibber and other Hands, *The Lives of the Poets of Great Britain and Ireland,* vol. 3 (London, 1753), 136–7.

presumably a comparable reflection of the most typical area of their author's social experience.[18] An important theatrical context is identified for us by Walpole's reference to 'genteel comedy'. This was the special term contemporaries frequently used when referring to that great sequence of comedies which form the prime achievement of the Restoration stage. 'The word *genteel* had at this time no sarcastic connotation, and Genteel Comedy was simply upper-class comedy'. The choice of title was, in part, a reflection of the rather proud conviction that the finest works of the post-1660 comic stage were characterized by a thoroughly authentic portrait of a much more socially elect range of characters than had been the case in earlier comedy.[19] According to John Downes, Robert Wilks, for whom Farquhar created the part of Archer, was an actor especially skilled in the intricate traditions of genteel comedy.[20] Writing a comic work for such a man and with the major achievements of the preceding forty years inevitably much in mind, Farquhar appears almost to have invited strictures of the kind eventually voiced by Cibber and Walpole. Quite apart from Sullen's tavern cronies and the responses they provoke, the text of Farquhar's play is crammed with passages of dialogue which serve to keep the question of what constitutes true gentility permanently in the audience's mind. Characters are continually eager to assert their right to the status of gentlefolk. This is the case even with Mrs Sullen, whose title to that rank might appear to be incontestable. Yet some lurking uneasiness in her mind surfaces explosively in her excessive reaction to a casual remark of Dorinda's: 'A maintenance! Do you take me, madam, for an hospital child, that I must sit down and bless my benefactors for meat, drink, and clothes?' (II.i, 19–21). Dorinda herself is exhilarated at the prospect of a marriage to Aimwell which will secure for her the regular tribute of all the outward and visible signs of 'place, and precedence' (IV.i, 412). I have already mentioned Cherry's earnest aspirations; as Archer puts it, she will be contented with 'nothing under a gentleman' for her husband (II.ii, 8–9). Similarly, Scrub solemnly swears to the truth of something 'upon my honour, as I'm a gentleman' (III.iii, 5), while Gipsy, definitely thinking of herself as made of better stuff, comments loftily upon the lack of civility habitually displayed by the common people of England to strangers (IV.i, 206–7). For Gibbet, a man's inherent gentility can be demonstrated even in the way in which he commits a robbery: 'there's a great deal of address and good

---

[18] *The Letters of Horace Walpole Fourth Earl of Orford*, ed. Peter Cunningham, vol. 9 (Edinburgh, 1906), 96.

[19] F. W. Bateson, 'Contributions to a Dictionary of Critical Terms 1. Comedy of Manners', *Essays in Criticism*, vol. 1 (1951), 91–2.

[20] John Downes, *Roscius Anglicanus* (London, 1708), p.51.

manners in robbing a lady; I am the most a gentleman that way that ever travelled the road' (IV.ii, 137–9). Boniface, far from finding Gibbet's logic eccentric, offers an extremist variation upon it; in his view, Aimwell 'is so much a gentleman every manner of way, that he must be a highwayman' (II.ii, 58–9).

In the complicated social structure of eighteenth-century England,

> The term gentleman marked the exact point at which the traditional social system divided up the population into two extremely unequal sections. About a twenty-fifth, at most a twentieth, of all the people alive in the England of the Tudors and the Stuarts . . . belonged to the gentry and to those above them in the social hierarchy. This tiny minority owned most of the wealth, wielded the power and made all the decisions, political, economic and social for the national whole.[21]

Farquhar's play carefully charts some of the ways in which the lives of the few were ordered by rules different from those which governed the many. Whatever high-flown airs he may on occasion allow himself, the lowliness of Scrub's lot is firmly documented for us by his own remarks on 'that same Pressing Act', which has effectively deprived servants of the wages due to them and dangles permanently over their heads, if they contemplate even muted protest, the dreaded prospect of 'being sent for a soldier' (III.iii, 50–1). In the next scene, Farquhar neatly introduces us to the French count, a soldier and prisoner-of-war, but released on parole in Lichfield and gaily devoting his unused energies to making love to Mrs Sullen. This he can do in some comfort, since, as Boniface has already told us, the enemy officers in town are 'full of money, and pay double for everything they have' (I.i, 106–7). The difference in styles of life which separates gentlemen from the rest could not be more succinctly delineated.

Yet, although the play leaves us in little doubt about the absurdity of Scrub's daydreaming, the situation with some of the other characters is rather more complex. Archer, in his disguise as a servant, prompts Scrub to repeated gasps of wonder and the heartfelt exclamation that 'he's clear another sort of man than I' (III.i, 71–2). Cherry's thoughts have already pursued a similar line, and she nimbly outmanoeuvres her would-be lover by informing him that 'your discourse and your habit are contradictions, and it would be nonsense in me to believe you a footman any longer' (II.ii, 185–7). Archer returns the compliment and deduces from Cherry's somewhat extravagant behaviour that 'she has better blood in her veins' than any she can owe to Boniface (II.ii, 3). Yet, while the play's ending has Archer returning to London with his status as gentleman newly restored, no comparable promotion is allowed to Cherry, who had

[21] Peter Laslett, *The World We Have Lost* (London, 1965), p. 26.

earlier proclaimed that, 'though I was born to servitude, I hate it' (II.ii, 190). Archer himself, whom she had hoped to marry (thus escaping her present fate), benignly arranges for her to remain in 'servitude', though now in the employment of Dorinda. Archer's attitude towards Cherry displays some interestingly quirky contradictions. Thus, he accepts unprotestingly the justice of those dubious laws of London society by which the 'professed pickpocket' who 'makes a handsome figure' can gain acceptance in the most select and elevated circles; yet, when he is offered two thousand pounds as a wedding dowry with Cherry, even the formidable pressure exerted by his desperate financial straits is insufficient to overcome some residual stirrings of social distaste: 'an innkeeper's daughter! ay, that's the devil—there my pride brings me off' (II.ii, 233–4). But, as Cherry herself has already acutely observed, such scruples are odd and inconsistent in a gentleman who has been calmly prepared to 'bear the scandal of wearing a livery' (II.ii, 216–17).[22] Archer's pride in his true rank is permitted only a highly selective and erratic expression. Similarly, although we can all agree that Archer's behaviour reveals him to be 'clear another sort of man than' Scrub, the play contrives to cast doubt upon whether the difference involved is revelatory of any inherent gentility in the gallant. Dorinda, for example, remembers that she has 'known several footmen come down from London set up here for dancing-masters, and carry off the best fortunes in the country' (III.iii, 111–13)—a scheme that Archer proclaims to be better than the one the beaux are currently operating. Dorinda's comment pinpoints for us just how much of Archer's impressiveness would, in fact, lie within the potential repertoire of such a talented and resourceful footman. This unworthy thought is echoed, and confirmed, by Archer's own choice of words when he tells Aimwell that, to drive the affair with Mrs Sullen to a successful climax, it will be necessary for him to 'put on the gentleman' (IV.ii, 39). So much of what is most attractive and beguiling in Archer's behaviour is of a piece with those things which immediately engage Scrub's attention on a first encounter with him; the wittily genteel manners and airs are as much the disposable props of his stratagem as the 'silver-headed cane' and the 'fine long periwig tied up in a bag' (III.i, 68, 70–1).

At one point, Mrs Sullen informs Dorinda that she has heard Sir Charles 'talk of my Lord Aimwell, but they say that his brother is the finer gentleman' (III.iii, 97–8). That judgement was presumably reached in the days of relative prosperity, before the beaux' 'friends

---

[22] For one contemporary's notion of how separate the worlds of gentleman and servant are, and ought to be, see John Locke, *Some Thoughts Concerning Education*, ed. Rev. R. H. Quick (Cambridge, 1902), p. 45.

... began to suspect that our pockets were low' (I.i, 172–3); then Sir Charles could bring himself to praise the less privileged brother at the expense of the elder. Aimwell and Archer can now expect from this 'proud knight' nothing better than 'to be despised, exposed, and laughed at' (V.iv, 60). In talking to Dorinda, Aimwell offers a tersely eloquent account of a younger brother's true history and status, which omits as irrelevant all pretensions to gentility: 'I am no lord, but a poor, needy man, come with a mean, a scandalous design to prey upon your fortune' (V.iv, 26–7). In addition to Aimwell, two other characters identify themselves (perhaps deceitfully) as younger brothers—Archer in talking to Cherry (II.ii, 195–6) and Gibbet while robbing the ladies (V.ii, 127). The plight of younger sons under primogeniture had been a topic of sustained and frequently urgent debate throughout the preceding century. During the period of the Interregnum, the Diggers had even 'turned the terms "elder brother" and "younger brother" into synonyms for the propertied, and unpropertied classes'. The dire dilemmas which afflicted younger brothers were closely connected to those intriguing questions of status which the histories of Archer and of Cherry prompt us to explore. A younger brother 'was born a gentleman', educated as a gentleman, 'expected to play the role of a gentleman, but lacked the wherewithal'.[23] His frequently unenviable fate indicated graphically how much his society tended, in the final analysis, to award the accolade of gentility to those who possessed the necessary financial recommendation, and was inclined to disregard, unless unaccompanied by such a recommendation, the claims of birth and of those moral and social qualities which were still, by common consent, regarded as intrinsically 'genteel' and 'generous'.[24] Certainly, in her moment of anger with Dorinda, Mrs Sullen assumes that her society's priorities are of this kind; she is clear that what finally separates her from the 'hospital child' is not the length of her family tree or any especially distinguished qualities of mind or spirit she may personally possess, but the fact that marriage to her brought the squire ten thousand pounds (II.i, 22). Not all the sums mentioned in the play are quite so impressive, but the formidable influence of money upon the characters' lives and world is patiently detailed in incident after incident. Scrub's life, for example, is greatly

[23] Joan Thirsk, 'Younger Sons in the Seventeenth Century', *History*, vol. 54 (1969), 369n, 360.
[24] For a very useful account of the extent to which Restoration and early eighteenth-century theorists made 'virtue the very source of nobility and gentility', see George C. Brauer, Jr, *The Education of a Gentleman: Theories of Gentlemanly Education in England, 1660–1775* (New York, 1959), p. 13 and passim.

simplified by the two guineas he receives from Archer; if the worst should happen, these will be sufficient to buy him off from the recruiting officer (IV.i, 364–5). Gibbet's escape from the hangman will depend upon his possession of a larger amount, two hundred pounds (V.ii, 155). In a typically revealing touch, the same sum (this time in Aimwell's strongbox) leads Cherry to assume automatically that the beau is a parliamentary candidate on a vote-buying tour (I.i, 282). Squire Sullen, echoing his wife's sense of what matters most in this society, is sharply aware of the freedoms which are the privileges of 'a man of a great estate'. Rebuked by his sister for 'being drunk last night', he ignores her criticism of his treatment of his wife and simply retorts: 'I can afford it, can't I?' (II.i, 93–4). The final act brings Sullen face to face with the only other Englishman in the play who throughout appears to be of assured and stable wealth. As Boniface (so often our guide in such matters) informs us, Sir Charles is a 'great man, as the saying is, for he scorns to travel with other people' (V.i, 2–3). This London gentleman considers his brother-in-law's behaviour inadequately genteel and shivers with distaste at the innkeeper's recital of the list of Sullen's drinking-companions: 'the constable, Mr. Gauge the exciseman, the hunchbacked barber, and two or three other gentlemen' (V.i, 11–12). Yet the right of Sir Charles to make such lofty judgements is not unassailable; similarities are once again being established between the ways of the town and of the country, since a man whose respect for Aimwell's gentility lasted only as long as the latter's solvency has more in common with the coarse-grained squire than he may care to admit.

The preoccupations I have been tracing in *The Beaux' Stratagem* were of more than intellectual interest to Farquhar. According to one authoritative biographer, 'Mr. *George Farquhar* was born, in the North of *Ireland*, of Parents that held no mean Rank in that Part of the Country; who, having a Numerous Issue, could bestow on him no other Fortune than a genteel Education'.[25] Again, in the last winter of his life, Farquhar is reported to have imitated the comic heroes he was soon to create and, without 'one Shilling in his Pocket', withdrew from his normal haunts and any contact with former friends and acquaintances. Unlike the beaux, however, he embarked upon no rural stratagems, but was eventually discovered by the faithful Wilks 'in a most miserable situation, lodged in a back garret, and under the greatest agitation of mind'.[26] At the actor's instigation, he began the writing of *The Beaux' Stratagem*. This 'last Comedy he wrote in six Weeks, with a settled Illness all the Time. He perceived the Approaches of Death before he had finish'd

---

[25] Chetwood, op. cit., p. 148.
[26] Rothstein, op. cit., p. 27. The quoted words are Colley Cibber's.

the last Act, and (as he had often foretold) died before the Run of the play was over'.[27] In an eloquent phrase, his widow was later to speak of his 'Lingring and Expensive Sickness'.[28] His comedy earned him the princely sum of thirty pounds from a publisher.[29] The principal characters in *The Beaux' Stratagem* play for rather more substantial stakes. Of great significance to them all is the figure of ten thousand pounds. This is the amount that Archer and Aimwell have already spent in London; it is also the amount of Mrs Sullen's dowry and of Dorinda's fortune. Not only is it a sum extravagantly beyond any that their creator can himself ever have handled; but, on the calculations of John Loftis, Farquhar has taken the liberty of bestowing upon his heiresses fortunes decidedly more generous than any their real-life counterparts would have been likely to enjoy.[30] There is a serious purpose behind this munificence. In a society where status is so intimately dependent upon wealth, even sums of this glamorous magnitude, the play argues, cannot offer their possessors any real assurance of truly lasting security. At the end of the play, Mrs Sullen is clearly likely to return to the town from which she came and whose praises she has so ardently sung; yet living in the capital has already cost the beaux a sum exactly equal to all she now possesses. The carefully identical amounts involved invite us to wonder how long, in London, it would be before the gap which separates the 'fine lady' from the 'hospital child' began to shrink drastically. But, even if Mrs Sullen forgoes the delights of the metropolis, she will not necessarily be secure. Gibbet has earlier told us the significant tale of 'a poor lady just eloped from her husband', from whom he has stolen that sum of two hundred pounds which may be of so much importance to his own survival. His compassion had been aroused, and he had kindly left her half a crown (II.ii, 74 ff.). It is not only real highwaymen that threaten the future of ladies just eloped from their husbands. An intricate sequence of comparisons between Gibbet's gang and the beaux carefully reminds the audience that 'Aimwell and Archer are also gentlemen who travel the roads of England in search of a lady's fortune'.[31]

[27] Chetwood, op. cit., p. 150.
[28] James R. Sutherland, 'New Light on George Farquhar', *The Times Literary Supplement*, 6 March 1937, p. 171.
[29] John Nichols (ed.), *Literary Anecdotes of the Eighteenth Century*, vol. 8 (London, 1814), 296.
[30] John Loftis, *Comedy and Society from Congreve to Fielding* (Stanford, California, 1959), pp. 46 ff.
[31] Alan Roper, '*The Beaux' Stratagem*: Image and Action', in Earl Miner (ed.), *Seventeenth-Century Imagery: Essays on Uses of Figurative Language from Donne to Farquhar* (Berkeley, Los Angeles and London, 1971), p.185.

The freedom Mrs Sullen has gained—founded, as it is, upon so assailable and purloinable a basis as the sum of ten thousand pounds —is of an alarmingly fragile nature.

Farquhar does not, however, prescribe that all his characters' actions should be directed by the demands of financial prudence. Indeed, Aimwell, in confessing his imposture to Dorinda, is made to act very decisively against what appear to be his own interests. The lady, however, is moved by an action she significantly dubs 'generous' and, paying tribute to the 'gentleman's honour', remains willing to marry him (V.iv, 89–90). This moment, and its sequel (the revelation that Aimwell has, in fact, become the nobleman he impersonated), are aspects of the play which many of its apologists, sensing an awkward surrender to sentimentality, have tended to handle uneasily and somewhat censoriously. In my view, however, Farquhar's wryly humane scepticism remains spry and active until the end. It is true that, at the actual moment of Aimwell's confession, Dorinda explicitly turns her back on her earlier preoccupation with the delights of 'place, and precedence': 'Once I was proud, sir, of your wealth and title, but now am prouder that you want it: now I can show my love was justly levelled, and had no aim but love' (V.iv, 36–9). But one prime effect of the news Sir Charles brings is that Dorinda's new-found dedication to love without an estate never has to be put to the test. Aimwell's unselfishness in telling her the truth is clearly an action radically untypical of that town world, of which he has hitherto been so enamoured, and of whose mores his elder brother is so apt a representative. Yet the way in which Dorinda announces the happy turn his fortunes have now taken suggests that such crucial distinctions have been pushed to the back of her mind by recent events; what makes her so ecstatic (as her rapt repetition of it makes evident) is his sudden acquisition of a title, and the 'place, and precedence' this will bring with it: 'you are the person that you thought you counterfeited; you are the true Lord Viscount Aimwell, and I wish your lordship joy.—Now, priest, you may be gone; if my lord is pleased now with the match, let his lordship marry me in the face of the world' (V.iv, 92–6). In the play's first scene, one of the beaux had bravely proclaimed that 'we are the men of intrinsic value, who can strike our fortunes out of ourselves, whose worth is independent of accidents in life, or revolutions in government'(I.i, 156–8); but, in the last scene, the fortuitous death which assures them of their happy ending is gratefully hailed (in a careful verbal echo) by the other beau thus: 'Thanks to the pregnant stars that formed this accident' (V.iv, 106). In this world, a man's value owes much more to his extrinsic than to his intrinsic qualities, and the dramatist gives us no leave to assume that the match between Dorinda and Aimwell constitutes a real exception to this rule.

Thus, *The Beaux' Stratagem* is a very deliberate contribution to the rich tradition of genteel comedy, but a contribution which determinedly brings into question many of its audience's more automatic assumptions about what actually constitutes true gentility —assumptions which, we may guess from their remarks, were shared by Walpole and Cibber. The latter's pious wish that Farquhar could have been enabled, by 'mingling with persons of rank', to write 'a more polish'd dialogue', reveals a desire to sustain a belief in precisely those truisms against which Farquhar directs some of his heaviest fire.

Richly interacting with the play's meditations upon the nature of gentility is its response to another topic which prompted much contemporary discussion. In 1924, Martin A. Larson conclusively demonstrated that substantial passages in the characters' debates on marriage and divorce were derived from Milton's great, and intensely controversial, pamphlet *The Doctrine and Discipline of Divorce* (first published in 1643). There is a certain piquancy in the sight of a dramatist of this particular tradition finding an important part of his material in such an apparently unlikely source, but, ironically, many of those contemporaries who responded publicly to Milton's views on divorce described them in ways markedly similar to some of the choicest abuse bestowed upon Restoration comedy by hostile observers. In effectively advocating that divorce should be available on the grounds of mental and spiritual incompatibility, Milton was voicing ideas radically dissentient from the orthodoxy of his time, and the zealously censorious were swift to indict him.[32] One pamphleteer, for example, assailed this 'Tractate of divorce, in which the bonds are let loose to inordinate lust', and another was prompted to lament this 'licentious pamphlet throwne abroad in these lawless times': 'Wo is me, To what a passe is the world come that a Christian, pretending to Reformation, should dare to tender so loose a project to the publique?' The tale was soon being recounted of one Mrs Attaway, who had derived the justification for 'runing away with another womans husband' from her reading of Milton's obnoxious doctrines, and, equally early, the accusation is heard that Milton's concern with his subject was entirely selfish in motivation, and that the poet, 'being a little tormented with an ill chosen Wife, set forth the Doctrine of Divorce to be truly Evan-

[32] A thorough account of the situation is provided by John G. Halkett, *Milton and the Idea of Matrimony: A Study of the Divorce Tracts and 'Paradise Lost'* (New Haven and London, 1970).

gelical'.[33] A year after the first appearance of *The Beaux' Stratagem*, Swift could still approvingly remind his readers that, 'when *Milton* writ his Book of Divorces, it was presently rejected as an occasional Treatise; because every Body knew, he had a Shrew for his Wife'.[34] Similarly long-lived was the accusation of licentiousness; in 1698, John Toland, who was responsible for the reprinting of Milton's prose works in that year, was still staunchly having to argue that 'No Pretence can be drawn from this Opinion to favor Libertinism'.[35] The possibility of such objections had been anticipated by Milton himself, who had laboured to convince his readers that any objective eye would immediately discern that his treatise offered no comfort to 'the brood of Belial, the draff of men, to whom no liberty is pleasing, but unbridled and vagabond lust without pale or partition'.[36] According to Jeremy Collier (one of the fiercest enemies of Restoration comedy), it was precisely such a 'brood of Belial' that many contemporary dramatists had singled out for their audiences to admire and imitate: by the terms of the definition standard in the comedies of the period, he alleged, 'A fine Gentleman, is a fine Whoring, Swearing, Smutty, Atheistical Man'.[37] To many contemporary observers, therefore, an alliance between the dramatists and the Milton of the divorce tracts would have seemed a thoroughly logical step. The real nature of the Miltonic presence in Farquhar's comedy, however, is far more subtle and complex than any such rudimentary paradigm would lead one to anticipate.

It is, of course, Mrs Sullen who uses the Miltonic arguments with the greatest fervour and personal urgency, and she is quite confident that, in wishing to escape from her marriage with the squire, she is merely seeking to avail herself of the righteous remedies recommended by the benign approval of divine providence (III.iii, 399 ff.). Mrs Oldfield, who created the part, was unable to match this confidence and sent word to Farquhar that she 'thought he had dealt too freely with the Character of Mrs. *Sullen*, in giving her to *Archer* without a proper Divorce, which was not a Security for her Honour'.[38]

[33] J. Milton French (ed.), *The Life Records of John Milton* (New Brunswick, New Jersey, 1949–58), vol. 1, 356; vol. 2, 242, 145; vol. 5, 35.

[34] Jonathan Swift, 'Remarks upon a Book, intitled, the Rights of the Christian Church, &c.', *The Bickerstaff Papers and Pamphlets on the Church*, ed. Herbert Davis (Oxford, 1940), p. 67.

[35] John Toland, 'The Life of John Milton', in Helen Darbishire (ed.), *The Early Lives of John Milton* (London, 1932), p. 123.

[36] John Milton, 'The Doctrine and Discipline of Divorce', *Prose Works* (Bohn Edition: London, 1875), vol. III, 173.

[37] Jeremy Collier, *A Short View of the Immorality and Profaneness of the English Stage* (London, 1698), p. 143.

[38] Chetwood, op. cit., p. 151.

In view of the persistent strictures Milton's views had provoked, such a response to Mrs Sullen's behaviour cannot have been a surprise to Farquhar. In fact, he actually appears to invite his audience to ask some awkwardly probing questions about the lady's character and motivation which are very similar to those we have already seen Swift asking about Milton. Thus, although her thoughts, when arguing about matrimonial issues, are much preoccupied with 'Heaven's decree' (III.iii, 417) and the need to conform to it, her behaviour in the scene with the Country Woman offers us a glimpse of a rather different Mrs Sullen. Lady Bountiful is angered to discover her daughter-in-law deriving thoughtless amusement from 'the misfortunes of other people' (IV.i, 40–1) and rebukes her for self-centredness: 'your own misfortunes should teach you to pity others' (IV.i, 43-4). Behind this tart exchange lies a quite radical, and crucial, division between the two characters in their notions of the proper uses of riches. Mrs Sullen, always the fine lady from London, would certainly echo the beaux' definition of a just employment of available funds—'so much pleasure for so much money' (I.i, 186). Lady Bountiful's quite opposite instinct, however, is to expend half of her income 'in charitable uses for the good of her neighbours' (I.i, 70–1). There can be little doubt which of the two attitudes contemporaries would have considered the more religious. In the sternly condemnatory words of Isaac Barrow, 'the *gripple wretch*, who will bestow nothing on his poor brother for God's sake, is evidently an infidel, having none at all, or very heathenish conceits of God'.[39] In a sermon dedicated to winning from the rich some charity for the 'hospital child', John Sharp emphasizes that it is God's peremptory demand that the wealthy man 'must not live to himself alone'; 'if others be not advantaged by him, he is rich to no Purpose'.[40] Similarly, Archbishop Tillotson, analysing the parable of Lazarus and the rich man, explains that the latter's sin was 'that he made all to serve his own sensuality and luxury, without any consideration of the wants and necessities of others'.[41] Thus, the play presents us with the intriguing paradox that the lady, who is so scrupulously pious in mode of argument when marriage and divorce are being debated, evinces quite different instinctive allegiances and preferences in other aspects of her behaviour.

[39] Isaac Barrow, 'The Duty and Reward of Bounty to the Poor', *Works*, vol. 1 (London, 1741: 5th edition), 316.
[40] John Sharp, 'Sermon IV. Preached at The Spittle. On the Fourteenth of April, 1680', *Fifteen Sermons Preached on Several Occasions*, vol. 1 (London, 1729: 6th edition), 110–11.
[41] John Tillotson, 'Sermon LXXII. The Parable of the Rich Man and Lazarus', *Works*, vol. 1 (London, 1722: 3rd edition), 532.

Although she manages to avoid committing adultery with Archer during the course of the play, Mrs Sullen is clearly drawn towards him, and in this attraction lie the seeds of further paradoxes of a similar kind. Both beaux are consistently characterized as resolutely and self-awarely profane in life-style. For example, in a society where regular attendance at church was still (theoretically, at any rate) enforced by the threat of legal punishments, Aimwell's five-year absenteeism from such holy places is quite an emphatic declaration of irreligious tendencies (II.ii, 44). In the same way, he eventually goes to church during the play, not for any pious motives, but as a preliminary manoeuvre in a complicated campaign of seduction. While his friend is thus earnestly employed, Archer spends his time gleefully teaching Cherry a mock catechism (II.ii, 137). The same laughing misapplication of the language of piety is evident in his dialogue at other moments—as, for example, when he is striving to convince Mrs Sullen of the sincerity of his attachment to her and thus lure her into bed: 'no panting pilgrim, after a tedious, painful voyage, e'er bowed before his saint with more devotion' (V.ii, 49–50). One biographical anecdote suggests that this was an aspect of his characters to which Farquhar is liable to have been especially sensitive. Confronted by his Trinity tutor with the task of commenting upon the miracle of Christ's walking upon the waters, he is alleged to have spread shock and consternation among his superiors by impiously suggesting that an explanation of the incident might be found in the proverb—'He that is born to be hanged needs fear no drowning'.[42]

Given this strain in Archer's character, there is an interesting indecorum to be traced in his being able to attract and fascinate Mrs Sullen. Farquhar develops this idea further, and consequently, at some moments, Archer's dialogue comes to function almost as a direct parody of some of the lady's more solemnly enunciated statements. Thus, her gravest arguments about ways of alleviating her dire predicament are derived from Miltonic sources; Archer accordingly is allowed to indulge in a passage of quite agile, and thoroughly worldly, burlesque of Miltonic rhetoric (III.ii, 23 ff.). Similarly, Mrs Sullen's views on divorce derive from an earnestly reverent definition of nature, 'the first lawgiver', and its providentially ratified edicts (III.iii, 414). Correspondingly, Archer jovially and blasphemously rebukes those who fail to dedicate all their available resources to pursuing a life of sensual enjoyment as men who 'destroy the rights of nature, and disappoint the blessings

[42] David Erskine Baker, Isaac Reed, and Stephen Jones, *Biographica Dramatica; or, A Companion to the Playhouse*, vol. 1, Part 1 (London, 1812), 226.

of providence' (I.i, 211–12). 'Nature' was a word of peculiarly flexible application during this period, and the marquess of Halifax's attempt to differentiate between two opposed definitions of it neatly annotates the gap between the views held of it by Archer and by Mrs Sullen:

> All laws flow from that of Nature, and where that is not the foundation, they may be legally imposed but they will be lamely obeyed. By this Nature is not meant that which fools and libertines would misquote to justify their excesses; it is innocent and uncorrupted Nature, that which disposeth men to choose virtue without its being prescribed, and which is so far from inspiring ill thoughts into us, that we take pains to suppress the good ones it infuseth.[43]

But, as we have already seen, there were many contemporaries who claimed that the Miltonic arguments themselves were precisely those of a libertine, formulated 'to justify . . . [desired] excesses', and it is surely one effect of the paradoxes I have been tracing that the spectator is led to wonder whether some modified and humaner form of such a scepticism might not be justly applicable to Mrs Sullen. She clearly handles the Miltonic arguments with genuine gravity and sobriety, but to what level of her consciousness has belief in them actually penetrated? To what extent is her respect for them fuelled by the fact that general acceptance of them would offer her release from what otherwise appears to be a hopeless situation? The fact that so much of her other behaviour is inconsistent with this segment of it indicates, at the very least, that her espousal of these doctrines has been inadequately pondered and digested.

Central to her speeches, and to Milton's tracts, is an emphasis upon the radical and essentially private and elusive nature of those 'disaffections' and 'antipathies' which finally render particular marriages unsustainable (III.iii, 406–9). A corollary of this, of course, is stern criticism of a system of matrimonial law which restricts its attention to matters of comparatively superficial concern, providing solace in a case of 'transient injury' but averting its eyes from 'endless aversions . . . rooted' in the soul (III.iii, 412, 407–8). In the song he performs for the ladies, Archer is comparably reductive in his view of human relationships. For him, a sexual encounter is easily summarized and as easily terminated:

> When the lover his moments has trifled,
> The trifle of trifles to gain,
> No sooner the virgin is rifled,
> But a trifle shall part 'em again.   (III.iii, 199–202)

[43] George Savile, Marquess of Halifax, 'The Character of a Trimmer', *Complete Works*, ed. J. P. Kenyon (Harmondsworth, 1969), p. 51.

In Archer's world of trifles, those deeper pressures, delights, and pains, upon a full sense of which Milton's entire position depends, are slighted, ignored, even denied. Quite alien to the beau is the Miltonic delight in the hope of that 'sweet and gladsome society'[44] which is what marriage, in its ideal form, would be—a society whose unity would be founded upon a deeply-rooted, and mutually delighted, spiritual and mental harmony between the partners. Archer's world, in comparison, is entrenchedly individualistic and ultimately solitary. Strikingly, all the indications are that it is to this latter world that Mrs Sullen will eventually commit herself. The play's quite distinctive version of the ritual which concludes so many Restoration comedies has Archer significantly performing with a willing Mrs Sullen 'a country dance to the trifle that I sung today' (V.iv, 277–8). It appears that those instincts which draw her to Archer will finally win over those opposed qualities which have made her intermittently responsive to the powerful resonances of the Miltonic viewpoint. It is, perhaps, finally not unfair to say that those arguments have functioned for her in a way rather difficult to distinguish from the function of some of the cruder casuistry employed by other characters in the play. In particular, the effect of Foigard's devious logic upon a grateful Gipsy strikes a very relevant note: the latter sighs comfortably—'Methinks I'm so easy after an absolution, and can sin afresh with so much security, that I'm resolved to die a martyr to't' (IV.i, 255–7). Certainly, the Miltonic arguments have been used (along with other implements) by Mrs Sullen to secure the freedom to pursue a way of life of which Milton would have been rigorously disapproving. Such rigour is not part of Farquhar's tone, but he surely invites us to be wryly, but sympathetically, aware of the contradictions and paradoxes that everywhere characterize Mrs Sullen's progress through the play.

In a comparatively brief introduction of this kind, it would be hubristic to attempt to explore the full complexity of a play as rich as this; but perhaps enough has been said to establish how detailedly intelligent and resourceful the mind behind this work is. This is still far from being the accepted view of Farquhar's achievement. Too many critics still see him as a talented but muddled man, whose plays are uneasily caught between a declining Restoration tradition of realism and hard-headed irony and a developing eighteenth-century comedy of sentiment and benevolence. In the words of Louis Kronenberger, 'As a child of a transition, he was caught between two sets of antagonistic values; he necessarily formulated

[44] Milton, op. cit., vol. III, 194.

no harmonious values of his own'.[45] That portrait fits not at all the sense I have (and which I hope has been adequately substantiated here) of a man calmly and precisely in control of his materials and quite stable and distinctive in his view of them—a man, also, entirely adequate to the formidable task of talking directly and engagingly to that very diverse audience on themes which immediately and powerfully concerned them. It is mere justice that *The Beaux' Stratagem* was one of the most popular comedies in its own time and remains one of the most frequently revived eighteenth-century works today.

[45] Louis Kronenberger, *The Thread of Laughter: Chapters on English Stage Comedy from Jonson to Maugham* (New York, 1970), p. 183.

THE TEXT

THE COPY-TEXT FOR THE PRESENT EDITION is the Cambridge University Library copy of the first edition (referred to in the notes as Q). This appeared on 27 March 1707 (three weeks after the play's first performance) and is the only edition which was certainly published before the author's death.

The first edition prints only the first two lines of both of Archer's songs; in this edition, the missing passages have been supplied from *The Dramatick Works of Mr. George Farquhar* (London, 1736), vol. I, 15–16, 90–1.

Spelling and punctuation have been modernized throughout.

Quotations from Milton's divorce tracts are taken from the Bohn edition of his *Prose Works*, vol. III (London, 1875); this seemed the aptest choice, since this is the text used by Martin A. Larson in his investigation of the Miltonic influences upon the play (see below, p. xxxiv for full reference), and use of the same text here seemed likely to facilitate reference by readers to this important article.

FURTHER READING

Gellert Spencer Alleman, *Matrimonial Law and the Materials of Restoration Comedy* (Philadelphia, 1942).

Ronald Berman, 'The Comedy of Reason', *Texas Studies in Literature and Language*, vol. 7 (1965), 161–8.

Willard Connely, *Young George Farquhar: The Restoration Drama at Twilight* (London, 1949).

Verlyn Flieger, 'Notes on the Titling of George Farquhar's *The Beaux' Stratagem*', Notes and Queries, vol. 224 (1979), 21–3.

William Gaskill, 'Finding a Style for Farquhar', *Theatre Quarterly*, vol. 1, no. 1 (January–March 1971), 15–20.

Garland Jack Gravitt, 'A Primer of Pleasure: Neo-Epicureanism in Farquhar's *Beaux' Stratagem*', *Thoth*, vol. 12, no. 2 (1972), 38–49.

Robert D. Hume, 'Marital Discord in English Comedy from Dryden to Fielding', *Modern Philology*, vol. 74 (1976–77), 248–72.

Eugene Nelson James, *The Development of George Farquhar as a Comic Dramatist* (The Hague and Paris, 1972).

Robert John Jordan, 'George Farquhar's Military Career', *Huntington Library Quarterly*, vol. 37 (1973–74), 251–64.

Martin A. Larson, 'The Influence of Milton's Divorce Tracts on Farquhar's *Beaux' Stratagem*', *Publications of the Modern Language Association of America*, vol. 39 (1924), 174–8.

Peter Lewis, '*The Beaux' Stratagem* and *The Beggar's Opera*', Notes and Queries, vol. 226 (1981), 221–4.

John McVeagh, 'George Farquhar and Commercial England', *Studies on Voltaire and the eighteenth century*, vol. 217 (1983), 65–81.

Judith Milhous and Robert D. Hume, '*The Beaux' Stratagem*: A Production Analysis', *Theatre Journal*, vol. 34 (1982), 77–95, reprinted, in altered form, in Judith Milhous and Robert D. Hume, *Producible Interpretation: Eight English Plays 1675–1707* (Carbondale and Edwardsville, 1985).

Barry N. Olshen, '*The Beaux' Stratagem* on the Nineteenth Century London Stage', *Theatre Notebook*, vol. 28 (1974), 70–80.

J. P. W. Rogers, 'The Dramatist Vs. The Dunce: George Farquhar and John Oldmixon', *Restoration and Eighteenth-Century Theatre Research*, vol. 10 (1971), 53–8.

Alan Roper, '*The Beaux' Stratagem:* Image and Action', in Earl Miner (ed.), *Seventeenth-Century Imagery: Essays on Uses of Figurative Language from Donne to Farquhar* (Berkeley, Los Angeles and London, 1971), pp. 169–86.

Eric Rothstein, *George Farquhar* (New York, 1967).

William L. Sharp, 'Restoration Comedy: An approach to modern Production', *Drama Survey*, vol. 7 (1968–69), 69–86.

James Sutherland, 'New Light on George Farquhar', *The Times Literary Supplement*, 6 March 1937, p. 171.

THE
Beaux Stratagem.

A
COMEDY.

As it is Acted at the

QUEEN's THEATRE

IN THE

H AY-M A R K E T.

B Y
Her MAJESTY's Sworn Comedians.

Written by Mr. Farquhar, *Author of the* Recruiting-Officer.

LONDON:

Printed for BERNARD LINTOTT, at the *Crofs-Keys* next
Nando's Coffee-Houfe in *Fleetftreet.*

ADVERTISEMENT

The reader may find some faults in this play, which my illness prevented the amending of, but there is great amends made in the representation, which cannot be matched, no more than the friendly and indefatigable care of Mr. Wilks, to whom I chiefly owe the success of the play.   5

GEORGE FARQUHAR

1–2 *illness prevented the amending of* It is possible that Farquhar had in mind here quite substantial changes probably already made in the version being performed in the playhouse. 'The collected editions [of Farquhar's works], from 1728, print the scene with Count Bellair in Act III in italics, with the note that the role of the count was cut out after the first night, and that his part in Act V was given thereafter to Foigard'. (R. Morton, ' "Blot and Insert Where You Please" : The Fortunes of 18th Century Play Texts', in Paul Fritz and David Williams (eds.), *The Triumph of Culture: 18th Century Perspectives* (Toronto, 1972), pp. 128–9). A similar rearrangement appears to have been normal in nineteenth-century performances (see Barry N. Olshen, '*The Beaux' Stratagem* on the Nineteenth Century London Stage', *Theatre Notebook*, vol. 28 (1974), 71), and the practice has been continued in some modern productions, as, for example, in William Gaskill's 1970 staging of the play at the National Theatre.
4 *Mr. Wilks* Robert Wilks (1665–1732), a famous and richly talented actor and a close friend of the dramatist. He appeared in the first performances of six of Farquhar's comedies; among these roles were some of his greatest, and most lasting, successes.

DRAMATIS PERSONAE

Men

AIMWELL, ⎱ *two gentlemen of broken fortunes, the*	*Mr. Mills*
ARCHER, ⎰ *first as master, and the second as*	*Mr. Wilks*
servant	
COUNT BELLAIR, *a French officer, prisoner at*	*Mr. Bowman*
Lichfield	
SULLEN, *a country blockhead, brutal to his*	*Mr. Verbruggen*
wife	
FREEMAN, *a gentleman from London*	*Mr. Keen*
FOIGARD, *a priest, chaplain to the French officers*	*Mr. Bowen*
GIBBET, *a highwayman*	*Mr. Cibber*
HOUNSLOW, ⎰ *his companions*	
BAGSHOT, ⎱	

(handwritten annotations in margins: "Tom", "Seb" beside AIMWELL/ARCHER; "Crist" beside SULLEN; "Gipsy—", "Lady Bountiful — Jill")

AIMWELL, ARCHER The two names are connected with that rich vein of military imagery which is sustained throughout the play and serve to identify the beaux as (in amatory matters) expert, professional marksmen—a term which Archer later punningly applies to Aimwell (III.ii, 1). Also present, in Archer's name at any rate, is some play upon the idea of Cupid the bowman; perhaps Farquhar was thinking here of Milton's potent use of the story of 'Love [who was] born an archer aiming' in his grave account of 'this dark region here below, which is not Love's proper sphere' (*Prose Works*, 111, 194). Aimwell's name also clearly contains a prediction of those sparks of more humane ambition which eventually prompt his confession to Dorinda.

FREEMAN A doubly appropriate surname; Sir Charles comes to free his sister from a radically uncongenial marriage, but, as a result of his property and estate, he is also personally free to mould the pattern of his own life in a way which very few of the other characters can ever hope to emulate.

FOIGARD defender of the faith; as Aimwell later remarks, 'a very good name for a clergyman' (IV.ii, 44).

HOUNSLOW, BAGSHOT Their names derive from the two famous and forlorn heaths where highwaymen were well known to be particularly energetic in the pursuit of their calling; but, as is the case with their leader, these names may also contain a gloomy prediction of their ultimate fate on the gallows, since it was not unusual for eighteenth-century justice to execute punishment on the very spot where a crime had been committed.

5

BONIFACE, *landlord of the inn*   *Mr. Bullock*
SCRUB, *servant to Mr. Sullen*   *Mr. Norris*
[CHAMBERLAIN
TAPSTER
FELLOW
TRAVELLERS]

Women

LADY BOUNTIFUL, *an old civil country gentle-*   *Mrs. Powell*
                woman, that cures all her neighbours
                of all distempers, and foolishly fond
                of her son, Sullen
DORINDA, *Lady Bountiful's daughter*   *Mrs. Bradshaw*
MRS. SULLEN, *her daughter-in-law*   *Mrs. Oldfield*
GIPSY, *maid to the ladies*   *Mrs. Mills*
CHERRY, *the landlord's daughter in the inn*   *Mrs. Bicknell*
[COUNTRY WOMAN]

Scene *Lichfield*

BONIFACE 'His name is a token of his duplicity, since beside its etymology of
    doing good (Latin, *bonum facere*) float its English connotations of
    "bonny face," the handsome *appearance* of virtue'. (Eric Rothstein,
    George Farquhar (New York, 1967), pp. 153–4). As Rothstein also notes
    (p. 195), the name's association 'with the Popes might have acted to
    denigrate the name with the Protestant English, and also to link the
    innkeeper with the Catholic Bellair and "Foigard" '.
SCRUB His name is, of course, partly chosen to reflect his role in Squire
    Sullen's household as a menial servant, a drudge; but also relevant is
    another meaning of 'scrub'—'a low stunted tree'. Norris's lack of
    inches was frequently 'aimed at in the names of characters written for
    him' (Leo Hughes, *A Century of English Farce* (Princeton, New Jersey,
    1956), p. 180).

PROLOGUE
Spoken by Mr. Wilks

When strife disturbs, or sloth corrupts an age,
Keen satire is the business of the stage.
When the Plain Dealer writ, he lashed those crimes
Which then infested most—the modish times:
But now, when faction sleeps, and sloth is fled,   5
And all our youth in active fields are bred;
When through Great Britain's fair extensive round
The trumps of fame the notes of union sound;
When Anna's sceptre points the laws their course,
And her example gives her precepts force: 10
There scarce is room for satire; all our lays
Must be, or songs of triumph, or of praise.
But, as in grounds best cultivated tares
And poppies rise among the golden ears,

3 *Plain Dealer* William Wycherley (1640–1716)—the nickname derives
from the title of one of his own plays (first performed in 1676), which
John Dryden described as 'one of the most bold, most general, and
most useful satires which has ever been presented on the English
theatre' (*Of Dramatic Poesy and Other Critical Essays*, ed. George
Watson (London, 1962), vol. 1, 199). References to Wycherley's
rigorous honesty in decrying the follies of the times are frequent in the
prologues and epilogues of the period; Mary Pix, for example, speaks
of his 'Plain Dealing *Muse*' and the 'Stinging Truths' with which he
assaulted the complacency of audiences (prologue to *The Different
Widows: Or, Intrigue All-A-Mode* (London, [1703])).

6 *active fields* England was at war with France in the War of the Spanish
Succession (1702–13). Soldiers were important members of the
audience during the winter months (campaigns being still very much
seasonal affairs), and, accordingly, references to the war (mostly enthusiastic and rousingly patriotic) are common in contemporary playtexts.

8 *union* the union of the parliaments of England and Scotland, which was
accomplished on 6 March 1707, two days before the first performance
of Farquhar's play.

10 *her example* a decorous compliment to Queen Anne, alluding to the
crucial influence contemporary theory allotted to the personal example
of the monarch in shaping the moral and spiritual life of the nation. For
a more cautious comment on the same topic, see Jonathan Swift,
Bickerstaff Papers and Pamphlets on the Church, ed. Herbert Davis
(Oxford, 1940), p. 47.

Our products so, fit for the field or school,   15
Must mix with nature's favourite plant—a fool:
A weed that has to twenty summers ran,
Shoots up in stalk, and vegetates to man.
Simpling our author goes from field to field
And culls such fools as may diversion yield;   20
And, thanks to nature, there's no want of those,
For, rain or shine, the thriving coxcomb grows.
Follies tonight we show ne'er lashed before,
Yet such as nature shows you every hour;
Nor can the pictures give a just offence,   25
For fools are made for jests to men of sense.

19 *Simpling* seeking or gathering medicinal herbs
20 *culls* plucks
22 *coxcomb* a foolish person

THE BEAUX' STRATAGEM

Act I, Scene i

Scene, an inn
Enter BONIFACE *running*

BONIFACE

Chamberlain! Maid! Cherry! daughter Cherry! all asleep?
all dead?

Enter CHERRY *running*

CHERRY

Here, here! Why d'ye bawl so, father? D'ye think we have no
ears?

BONIFACE

You deserve to have none, you young minx! The company of   5
the Warrington coach has stood in the hall this hour, and
nobody to show them to their chambers.

CHERRY

And let 'em wait farther; there's neither red-coat in the
coach, nor footman behind it.

BONIFACE

But they threaten to go to another inn tonight.   10

CHERRY

That they dare not, for fear the coachman should overturn
them tomorrow.—Coming! coming!—Here's the London
coach arrived.

Enter several people with trunks, bandboxes, and other luggage,
and cross the stage

BONIFACE

Welcome, ladies!

---

  1 *Chamberlain* servant in charge of the bedrooms at an inn
13 s.d. *bandboxes* slight boxes of cardboard or very thin chip, for
    collars, hats, caps, and millinery

---

  6 *Warrington coach* Strauss remarks upon the difference in treatment
meted out to the passengers from the local coach (Warrington being
about 60 miles from Lichfield) and those arriving from the more
glamorous metropolis.
11–12 *overturn them tomorrow* It was well known that coachmen received
bribes from innkeepers for making regular stops at particular establish-
ments; if compelled by his passengers to bypass one of these halts, a
coachman could be relied upon to exact an exemplary revenge.

CHERRY
Very welcome, gentlemen!—Chamberlain, show the Lion   15
and the Rose.   *Exit with the company*

Enter AIMWELL *in riding habit,* ARCHER *as footman carrying a portmantle*

BONIFACE
This way, this way, gentlemen!
AIMWELL
Set down the things; go to the stable, and see my horses well
rubbed.
ARCHER
I shall, sir.   *Exit*   20
AIMWELL
You're my landlord, I suppose?
BONIFACE
Yes, sir, I'm old Will Boniface, pretty well known upon this
road, as the saying is.
AIMWELL
O Mr. Boniface, your servant!
BONIFACE
O sir!—What will your honour please to drink, as the saying   25
is?
AIMWELL
I have heard your town of Lichfield much famed for ale; I
think I'll taste that.
BONIFACE
Sir, I have now in my cellar ten tun of the best ale in
Staffordshire; 'tis smooth as oil, sweet as milk, clear as   30
amber, and strong as brandy; and will be just fourteen year
old the fifth day of next March, old style.
AIMWELL
You're very exact, I find, in the age of your ale.
BONIFACE
As punctual, sir, as I am in the age of my children. I'll show

15–16 *the Lion and the Rose* the names of rooms in the inn
16 s.d. *habit* dress
16 s.d. *portmantle* portmanteau
29 *tun* a cask or barrel, containing 252 old wine-gallons

32 *old style* According to the Julian calendar, still in use in Britain. It had
been replaced in the rest of western Europe by the Gregorian or New
Style Calendar; by 1700, the latter was eleven days ahead of the Julian.

you such ale!—Here, tapster, broach number 1706, as the   35
saying is.—Sir, you shall taste my *Anno Domini*.—I have
lived in Lichfield, man and boy, above eight and fifty years,
and, I believe, have not consumed eight and fifty ounces of
meat.

AIMWELL

At a meal, you mean, if one may guess your sense by your   40
bulk.

BONIFACE

Not in my life, sir; I have fed purely upon ale; I have eat my
ale, drank my ale, and I always sleep upon ale.

Enter tapster with a bottle and glass

Now, sir, you shall see!—(*Filling it out*) Your worship's
health.—Ha! delicious, delicious—fancy it burgundy, only   45
fancy it, and 'tis worth ten shillings a quart.

AIMWELL (*Drinks*)

'Tis confounded strong.

BONIFACE

Strong! It must be so, or how should we be strong that
drink it?

AIMWELL

And have you lived so long upon this ale, landlord?   50

BONIFACE

Eight and fifty years, upon my credit, sir; but it killed my
wife, poor woman, as the saying is.

AIMWELL

How came that to pass?

BONIFACE

I don't know how, sir; she would not let the ale take its
natural course, sir; she was for qualifying it every now and   55
then with a dram, as the saying is; and an honest gentleman
that came this way from Ireland made her a present of a
dozen bottles of usquebaugh—but the poor woman was

35 *tapster* man who draws ale for customers at an inn
43 s.d. *glass* glassware
56 *dram* a small draught of spirits
58 *usquebaugh* whiskey

35 *number 1706* If Boniface's *Anno Domini* is numbered by its year, then it
is only one year old and not fourteen.
41 *bulk* Cf. one contemporary writer's observation that, in standard stage
practice, 'Swol'n Cheeks, and swagging Bellies, make an *Host*' (Emmett
L. Avery, 'A Poem on Dorset Garden Theatre', *Theatre Notebook*, vol.
18 (1963–64), 123).

never well after. But, howe'er, I was obliged to the gentleman,
you know.   60
AIMWELL
Why, was it the usquebaugh that killed her?
BONIFACE
My Lady Bountiful said so. She, good lady, did what
could be done; she cured her of three tympanies, but the
fourth carried her off. But she's happy, and I'm contented,
as the saying is.   65
AIMWELL
Who's that Lady Bountiful you mentioned?
BONIFACE
Ods my life, sir, we'll drink her health. (*Drinks*) My Lady
Bountiful is one of the best of women. Her last husband, Sir
Charles Bountiful, left her worth a thousand pound a
year; and, I believe, she lays out one half on't in charitable   70
uses for the good of her neighbours. She cures rheumatisms,
ruptures, and broken shins in men; green-sickness, obstruc-
tions, and fits of the mother in women; the king's evil, chin-
cough, and chilblains in children; in short, she has cured
more people in and about Lichfield within ten years than   75
the doctors have killed in twenty; and that's a bold word.
AIMWELL
Has the lady been any other way useful in her generation?
BONIFACE
Yes, sir; she has a daughter by Sir Charles, the finest woman
in all our country, and the greatest fortune. She has a son
too, by her first husband, Squire Sullen, who married a fine   80

63 *tympanies* an 'obstructed flatulence that swells the body like a
   drum' (Dr Johnson's Dictionary)
72 *green-sickness* chlorosis, an anaemic disease which mostly affects
   young women about the age of puberty
73 *fits of the mother* hysteria
73 *king's evil* scrofula, a disease which, it was believed, could be
   cured by the touch of the monarch's hand
73–4 *chin-cough* whooping cough
79 *country* region or county

76 *doctors have killed* In *The Recruiting Officer* (II.ii), Farquhar gives the
   name of Killman to the offstage doctor who attends Justice Balance's
   dying son.
77 *useful in her generation* The neatest variation on this favourite
   Restoration formula is given by Congreve in *The Double Dealer* (III.ii)
   to the elderly Sir Paul Plyant: 'alas! what's once a year to an old man,
   who would do good in his generation?'

lady from London t'other day; if you please, sir, we'll drink
his health.

AIMWELL

What sort of a man is he?

BONIFACE

Why, sir, the man's well enough; says little, thinks less, and
does—nothing at all, faith. But he's a man of a great estate,   85
and values nobody.

AIMWELL

A sportsman, I suppose.

BONIFACE

Yes, sir, he's a man of pleasure; he plays at whisk, and
smokes his pipe eight and forty hours together sometimes.

AIMWELL

And married, you say?   90

BONIFACE

Ay, and to a curious woman, sir. But he's a—he wants it here,
sir. (*Pointing to his forehead*)

AIMWELL

He has it there, you mean?

BONIFACE

That's none of my business; he's my landlord, and so a man,
you know, would not—But—ecod, he's no better than—   95
Sir, my humble service to you.—(*Drinks*) Though I value
not a farthing what he can do to me; I pay him his rent at
quarter-day; I have a good running trade; I have but one
daughter, and I can give her—but no matter for that.

AIMWELL

You're very happy, Mr. Boniface. Pray, what other company   100
have you in town?

88 *whisk* the earlier name of the card-game now called whist
91 *curious* probably, strange or singular; but Boniface may also be
    thinking of another of this adjective's meanings—fastidious or
    difficult to satisfy
98 *quarter-day* one of the four days of the year fixed for payment of
    rent
98 *running* yielding a steady income

---

87 *A sportsman* Cf. Defoe's tart question: 'Do not we English gentlemen
    think, that to be a good sportsman is the perfeccion of education, and to
    speak good dog language and good horse language is far abov Greek
    and Latin?' (*The Compleat English Gentleman*, ed. Karl D. Bülbring
    (London, 1890), p. 38.)
91–3 *wants it here . . . has it there* Boniface means that the squire is stupid;
    Aimwell implies that Sullen bears cuckold's horns upon his forehead.

BONIFACE
   A power of fine ladies; and then we have the French officers.
AIMWELL
   O, that's right; you have a good many of those gentlemen.
   Pray, how do you like their company?
BONIFACE
   So well, as the saying is, that I could wish we had as many   105
   more of 'em; they're full of money, and pay double for every-
   thing they have. They know, sir, that we paid good round
   taxes for the taking of 'em, and so they are willing to reim-
   burse us a little. One of 'em lodges in my house.

                    Enter ARCHER

ARCHER
   Landlord, there are some French gentlemen below that ask   110
   for you.
BONIFACE
   I'll wait on 'em.—(*To* ARCHER) Does your master stay long in
   town, as the saying is?
ARCHER
   I can't tell, as the saying is.
BONIFACE
   Come from London?   115
ARCHER
   No.
BONIFACE
   Going to London, mayhap?
ARCHER
   No.
BONIFACE
   An odd fellow this!—I beg your worship's pardon; I'll wait
   on you in half a minute.   *Exit*   120
AIMWELL
   The coast's clear, I see. Now, my dear Archer, welcome
   to Lichfield!
ARCHER
   I thank thee, my dear brother in iniquity.
AIMWELL
   Iniquity! prithee, leave canting; you need not change your
   style with your dress.   125

102 *power* a large number
124 *canting* making a hypocritical use of religious vocabulary
_____

102 *the French officers* During the War of the Spanish Succession some
   captured officers were released on parole in various English towns.

ARCHER

Don't mistake me, Aimwell, for 'tis still my maxim, that
there is no scandal like rags, nor any crime so shameful as
poverty.

AIMWELL

The world confesses it every day in its practice, though men
won't own it for their opinion. Who did that worthy lord, my   130
brother, single out of the side-box to sup with him t'other
night?

ARCHER

Jack Handicraft, a handsome, well-dressed, mannerly,
sharping rogue, who keeps the best company in town.

AIMWELL

Right! And, pray, who married my Lady Manslaughter   135
t'other day, the great fortune?

ARCHER

Why, Nick Marrabone, a professed pickpocket, and a good
bowler; but he makes a handsome figure, and rides in his
coach, that he formerly used to ride behind.

AIMWELL

But did you observe poor Jack Generous in the park last   140
week?

ARCHER

Yes, with his autumnal periwig shading his melancholy face,
his coat older than anything but its fashion, with one hand

134 *sharping* cheating
140 *Generous* of noble lineage, high-born
140 *the park* St James's Park

---

131 *side-box* box at the side of the theatre, where people of fashion
    sometimes came to be seen by the other people in the house rather than
    to watch the play (Rothstein).
137 *Nick* In the light of the other information we are given about him, this
    character bears a doubly appropriate Christian name; as a verb, 'nick'
    could mean (1) to cheat, defraud and (2) to gamble.
137 *Marrabone* a corruption of Marylebone, an area of London which
    numbered among its famous (and, to some, notorious) attractions a
    bowling-green and gambling-houses. (For an account of the changes
    rung upon the place's name, see R. E. Zachrisson, 'Marylebone—-
    Tyburn—Holborn', *Modern Language Review*, vol. 12 (1917), 146–56.)
137–8 *a good bowler* His sporting talents clearly explain Farquhar's choice
    of surname (see note above). To illustrate a current proverbial connec-
    tion between bowling and criminality, Jeffares usefully cites Francis
    Quarles's 'The vulgar Proverb's crost: he can hardly be a good Bowler
    and an Honest man' (*Emblemes*, 1635, I, x).

idle in his pocket, and with the other picking his useless
teeth; and though the Mall was crowded with company, yet   145
was poor Jack as single and solitary as a lion in a desert.

AIMWELL

And as much avoided, for no crime upon earth but the want
of money.

ARCHER

And that's enough. Men must not be poor; idleness is the
root of all evil; the world's wide enough, let 'em bustle.   150
Fortune has taken the weak under her protection, but men
of sense are left to their industry.

AIMWELL

Upon which topic we proceed, and, I think, luckily hitherto.
Would not any man swear now that I am a man of quality,
and you my servant, when if our intrinsic value were known—   155

ARCHER

Come, come, we are the men of intrinsic value, who can
strike our fortunes out of ourselves, whose worth is independent of accidents in life, or revolutions in government:
we have heads to get money and hearts to spend it.

AIMWELL

As to our hearts, I grant ye, they are as willing tits as any   160
within twenty degrees: but I can have no great opinion of our
heads from the service they have done us hitherto, unless it
be that they have brought us from London hither to Lichfield, made me a lord and you my servant.

ARCHER

That's more than you could expect already. But what money   165
have we left?

AIMWELL

But two hundred pound.

145 *the Mall* a walk bordered by trees in St James's Park, a place of
    promenade for the fashionable
150 *bustle* bestir themselves
154 *quality* rank
160 *tits* small horses, nags

149–50 *idleness is the root of all evil* Archer mischievously appropriates to
    impious uses a theme dear to contemporary Protestant clerics and
    moralists. In his *Of Industry*, for example, Isaac Barrow, the great
    Anglican preacher, asserts that 'in places where there is least work, the
    worst sins do most prevail; and idleness therefore was by the Prophet
    reckoned one of the great sins of Sodom, parents of the rest'; it only
    rarely happens 'that he who is idle, is not also dissolute' (*Works*, vol. 3
    (London, 1741: 5th edition), 165).

ARCHER

And our horses, clothes, rings, etc.—Why, we have very good
fortunes now for moderate people; and let me tell you besides, that this two hundred pound, with the experience that   170
we are now masters of, is a better estate than the ten thousand
we have spent.—Our friends, indeed, began to suspect that
our pockets were low; but we came off with flying colours,
showed no signs of want either in word or deed.

AIMWELL

Ay, and our going to Brussels was a good pretence enough   175
for our sudden disappearing; and, I warrant you, our
friends imagine that we are gone a-volunteering.

ARCHER

Why, faith, if this prospect fails, it must e'en come to that. I
am for venturing one of the hundreds, if you will, upon this
knight-errantry; but, in case it should fail, we'll reserve the   180
t'other to carry us to some counterscarp, where we may die as
we lived, in a blaze.

AIMWELL

With all my heart; and we have lived justly, Archer: we
can't say that we have spent our fortunes, but that we have
enjoyed 'em.   185

ARCHER

Right! so much pleasure for so much money. We have had
our pennyworths, and, had I millions, I would go to the same
market again.—O London, London!—Well, we have had
our share, and let us be thankful. Past pleasures, for aught I
know, are best, such as we are sure of; those to come may   190
disappoint us.

AIMWELL

It has often grieved the heart of me to see how some inhuman
wretches murder their kind fortunes; those that, by sacrific-
ing all to one appetite, shall starve all the rest. You shall
have some that live only in their palates, and in their sense   195
of tasting shall drown the other four: others are only

169–71 *besides* ed. (besides Thousand Q); *ten thousand* ed. (Ten Q)
177 *a-volunteering* i.e., for the army

---

181 *counterscarp* in fortification, the outer wall or slope of the ditch which
supports the covered way. Archer's general meaning is that they should
imitate the history of one of Farquhar's previous heroes, Captain
Plume, who had enlisted as a volunteer and served in the ranks for a
time. He, however, had eventually risen to command a company (see
The Recruiting Officer, II.iii).

epicures in appearances, such who shall starve their nights
to make a figure a days, and famish their own to feed the
eyes of others: a contrary sort confine their pleasures to the
dark, and contract their spacious acres to the circuit of a   200
muff-string.

ARCHER

Right! But they find the Indies in that spot where they con-
sume 'em, and I think your kind keepers have much the best
on't: for they indulge the most senses by one expense.
There's the seeing, hearing, and feeling, amply gratified; and   205
some philosophers will tell you, that from such a commerce
there arises a sixth sense, that gives infinitely more pleasure
than the other five put together.

AIMWELL

And to pass to the other extremity, of all keepers I think those
the worst that keep their money.   210

ARCHER

Those are the most miserable wights in being; they destroy the
rights of nature, and disappoint the blessings of providence.
Give me a man that keeps his five senses keen and bright as
his sword, that has 'em always drawn out in their just order
and strength, with his reason as commander at the head of 'em,   215
that detaches 'em by turns upon whatever party of pleasure
agreeably offers, and commands 'em to retreat upon the least
appearance of disadvantage or danger. For my part, I can
stick to my bottle, while my wine, my company, and my
reason, holds good; I can be charmed with Sappho's singing   220
without falling in love with her face; I love hunting, but
would not, like Actaeon, be eaten up by my own dogs; I love
a fine house, but let another keep it; and just so I love a fine
woman.

AIMWELL

In that last particular you have the better of me.   225

ARCHER

Ay, you're such an amorous puppy, that I'm afraid you'll

202 *Indies* the source of their delights (Nettleton and Case)
211 *wights* men

---

203 *kind keepers* men who keep mistresses. There was a notorious comedy
by John Dryden called *The Kind Keeper; or, Mr. Limberham* (first
performed in 1678) which had attracted the disapproving attention of
the licensing authorities.
222 *Actaeon* the young huntsman in Greek mythology who, because he saw
the goddess Diana bathing, was turned into a stag and hunted by his
own dogs.

spoil our sport; you can't counterfeit the passion without
feeling it.

AIMWELL

Though the whining part be out of doors in town, 'tis still in
force with the country ladies.—And let me tell you, Frank,　230
the fool in that passion shall outdo the knave at any time.

ARCHER

Well, I won't dispute it now; you command for the day,
and so I submit.—At Nottingham, you know, I am to be
master.

AIMWELL

And at Lincoln, I again.　　235

ARCHER

Then, at Norwich, I mount, which, I think, shall be our last
stage; for, if we fail there, we'll embark for Holland, bid
adieu to Venus, and welcome Mars.

AIMWELL

A match!—　　*end of scene*

***Enter* BONIFACE**

Mum!　　240

BONIFACE

What will your worship please to have for supper?

AIMWELL

What have you got?

BONIFACE

Sir, we have a delicate piece of beef in the pot, and a pig at the
fire.

AIMWELL

Good supper-meat, I must confess. I can't eat beef, landlord.　245

ARCHER

And I hate pig.

AIMWELL

Hold your prating, sirrah! Do you know who you are?

BONIFACE

Please to bespeak something else; I have everything in the
house.

AIMWELL

Have you any veal?　　250

229 *out of doors* out of fashion

---

229 *whining part* a term of almost technical status in Restoration discussions
of some of the more extreme manifestations of romantic love—see
David S. Berkeley, 'The Art of "Whining" Love', *Studies in Philology*,
vol. 52 (1955), 478–96.

BONIFACE
Veal! Sir, we had a delicate loin of veal on Wednesday last.

AIMWELL
Have you got any fish or wildfowl?

BONIFACE
As for fish, truly, sir, we are an inland town, and indifferently provided with fish, that's the truth on't; and then for wild-fowl—we have a delicate couple of rabbits.   255

AIMWELL
Get me the rabbits fricasseed.

BONIFACE
Fricasseed! Lard, sir, they'll eat much better smothered with onions.

ARCHER
Pshaw! Damn your onions!

AIMWELL
Again, sirrah!—Well, landlord, what you please. But hold,   260
I have a small charge of money, and your house is so full of strangers, that I believe it may be safer in your custody than mine; for when this fellow of mine gets drunk, he minds nothing.—Here, sirrah, reach me the strongbox.

ARCHER
Yes, sir.—(*Aside*) This will give us a reputation.   265
                                        Brings the box

AIMWELL
Here, landlord; the locks are sealed down both for your security and mine; it holds somewhat above two hundred pound: if you doubt it, I'll count it to you after supper. But be sure you lay it where I may have it at a minute's warning; for my affairs are a little dubious at present;   270
perhaps I may be gone in half an hour, perhaps I may be your guest till the best part of that be spent; and pray order your ostler to keep my horses always saddled. But one thing above the rest I must beg, that you would let this fellow have none of your *Anno Domini*, as you call it; for he's the   275
most insufferable sot.—Here, sirrah, light me to my chamber.
                                        Exit, lighted by ARCHER

BONIFACE
Cherry! daughter Cherry!

                    Enter CHERRY

CHERRY
D'ye call, father?

261 *charge of money* amount of money

BONIFACE
Ay, child, you must lay by this box for the gentleman: 'tis
full of money.   280
CHERRY
Money! all that money! Why, sure, father, the gentleman
comes to be chosen parliament-man. Who is he?
BONIFACE
I don't know what to make of him; he talks of keeping
his horses ready saddled, and of going perhaps at a minute's
warning, or of staying perhaps till the best part of this be   285
spent.
CHERRY
Ay, ten to one, father, he's a highwayman.
BONIFACE
A highwayman! Upon my life, girl, you have hit it, and
this box is some new-purchased booty. Now, could we find
him out, the money were ours.   290
CHERRY
He don't belong to our gang.
BONIFACE
What horses have they?
CHERRY
The master rides upon a black.
BONIFACE
A black! ten to one the man upon the black mare; and, since
he don't belong to our fraternity, we may betray him with   295
a safe conscience: I don't think it lawful to harbour any rogues
but my own.—Look ye, child, as the saying is, we must go
cunningly to work; proofs we must have. The gentleman's
servant loves drink, I'll ply him that way: and ten to one
loves a wench; you must work him t'other way.   300
CHERRY
Father, would you have me give my secret for his?
BONIFACE
Consider, child, there's two hundred pound to boot.—

289 *new-purchased* recently captured

---

282 *parliament-man* Bribery was common in the parliamentary elections of
the eighteenth century, votes being sold for cash or for liquor. Farquhar was writing in the middle of a period of particularly intense
political activity; 'more general elections, and more contests at these
elections, took place between 1689 and 1715 than for the rest of the
eighteenth century' (J. H. Plumb, *The Growth of Political Stability in
England 1675–1725* (Harmondsworth, 1969), pp. 10–11).

(*Ringing without*) Coming! coming!—Child, mind your
business.   [*Exit*]
CHERRY
What a rogue is my father! My father! I deny it. My   305
mother was a good, generous, free-hearted woman, and I
can't tell how far her good nature might have extended for the
good of her children. This landlord of mine, for I think I
can call him no more, would betray his guest, and debauch his
daughter into the bargain—by a footman too!   310

Enter ARCHER

ARCHER
What footman, pray, mistress, is so happy as to be the
subject of your contemplation?
CHERRY
Whoever he is, friend, he'll be but little the better for't.
ARCHER
I hope so, for I'm sure you did not think of me.
CHERRY
Suppose I had?   315
ARCHER
Why, then, you're but even with me; for the minute I came
in, I was a-considering in what manner I should make
love to you.
CHERRY
Love to me, friend!
ARCHER
Yes, child.   320
CHERRY
Child! Manners!—If you kept a little more distance, friend,
it would become you much better.
ARCHER
Distance! Good night, sauce-box.   *Going*
CHERRY
A pretty fellow! I like his pride.—Sir, pray, sir, you see, sir,
(ARCHER *returns*) I have the credit to be entrusted with   325
your master's fortune here, which sets me a degree above his
footman; I hope, sir, you an't affronted.
ARCHER
Let me look you full in the face, and I'll tell you whether you
can affront me or no.—'Sdeath, child, you have a pair of
delicate eyes, and you don't know what to do with 'em.   330

304 *business* Boniface is punning; the slang meaning of 'business' was
'sexual_intercourse'

CHERRY
Why, sir, don't I see everybody?
ARCHER
Ay, but if some women had 'em, they would kill everybody.
Prithee, instruct me; I would fain make love to you, but I
don't know what to say.
CHERRY
Why, did you never make love to anybody before?   335
ARCHER
Never to a person of your figure, I can assure you, madam:
my addresses have been always confined to people within my
own sphere; I never aspired so high before.   *A song*

But you look so bright,
And are dressed so tight,   340
That a man would swear you're right,
As arm was e'er laid over.
Such an air
You freely wear
To ensnare,   345
As makes each guest a lover:

Since then, my dear, I'm your guest,
Prithee give me of the best
Of what is ready dressed:
Since then, my dear, etc.   350

CHERRY
(*Aside*) What can I think of this man?—Will you give me that
song, sir?
ARCHER
Ay, my dear, take it while 'tis warm. (*Kisses her*) Death
and fire! her lips are honeycombs.
CHERRY
And I wish there had been bees too, to have stung you for   355
your impudence.
ARCHER
There's a swarm of Cupids, my little Venus, that has done
the business much better.
CHERRY
(*Aside*) This fellow is misbegotten as well as I.—What's
your name, sir?   360
ARCHER
(*Aside*) Name! egad, I have forgot it.—O! Martin.

336 *figure* elevated rank

CHERRY
  Where were you born?
ARCHER
  In St. Martin's parish.
CHERRY
  What was your father?
ARCHER
  St. Martin's parish.   365
CHERRY
  Then, friend, good night.
ARCHER
  I hope not.
CHERRY
  You may depend upon't.
ARCHER
  Upon what?
CHERRY
  That you're very impudent.   370
ARCHER
  That you're very handsome.
CHERRY
  That you're a footman.
ARCHER
  That you're an angel.
CHERRY
  I shall be rude.
ARCHER
  So shall I.   375
CHERRY
  Let go my hand.
ARCHER
  Give me a kiss.   *Kisses her*
  (*Call without*)
  Cherry! Cherry!
CHERRY
  I'mm—my father calls. You plaguy devil, how durst you stop
  my breath so?—Offer to follow me one step, if you dare.   380
                                                 [*Exit*]

365 *St. Martin's parish* An appropriate birthplace for Archer to lay claim to,
    it was well known as a centre for dealers in imitation jewellery. 'St.
    Martin's ware' had come to mean 'counterfeit goods'. There is an
    obvious significance in the fact that, in adopting the name of Martin
    (with all its devious associations), Archer is abandoning his true
    Christian name, Frank.

ARCHER
  A fair challenge, by this light! This is a pretty fair opening
  of an adventure: but we are knight-errants, and so Fortune
  be our guide.   *Exit*

Act II, [Scene i]

Scene, a gallery in LADY BOUNTIFUL's *house*
[Enter] MRS. SULLEN *and* DORINDA, *meeting*

DORINDA
  Morrow, my dear sister; are you for church this morning?
MRS. SULLEN
  Anywhere to pray; for Heaven alone can help me. But I
  think, Dorinda, there's no form of prayer in the liturgy
  against bad husbands.
DORINDA
  But there's a form of law in Doctors' Commons; and I swear,   5
  sister Sullen, rather than see you thus continually discontented, I would advise you to apply to that: for besides the
  part that I bear in your vexatious broils, as being sister to the
  husband, and friend to the wife, your example gives me such
  an impression of matrimony, that I shall be apt to condemn   10
  my person to a long vacation all its life. But supposing,
  madam, that you brought it to a case of separation, what
  can you urge against your husband? My brother is, first, the
  most constant man alive.
MRS. SULLEN
  The most constant husband, I grant ye.   15
DORINDA
  He never sleeps from you.
MRS. SULLEN
  No, he always sleeps with me.
DORINDA
  He allows you a maintenance suitable to your quality.

---

383 s.d. *Exit* Q follows this with '*The End of the First Act*'

  5 *Doctors' Commons* the college of the Doctors of the Civil Law in
    London, the activities of whose members included the handling of
    cases of divorce or separation in the ecclesiastical courts.
 11 *long vacation* i.e., the period during which there was a halt to all activity
    (including matrimonial cases) in the courts.

MRS. SULLEN

A maintenance! Do you take me, madam, for an hospital
child, that I must sit down and bless my benefactors for   20
meat, drink, and clothes? As I take it, madam, I brought
your brother ten thousand pounds, out of which I might
expect some pretty things called pleasures.

DORINDA

You share in all the pleasures that the country affords.

MRS. SULLEN

Country pleasures! Racks and torments! Dost think, child,   25
that my limbs were made for leaping of ditches, and
clambering over stiles? or that my parents, wisely fore-
seeing my future happiness in country pleasures, had early
instructed me in the rural accomplishments of drinking fat
ale, playing at whisk, and smoking tobacco with my husband;   30
or of spreading of plaisters, brewing of diet-drinks, and
stilling rosemary-water, with the good old gentlewoman my
mother-in-law?

DORINDA

I'm sorry, madam, that it is not more in our power to divert
you; I could wish, indeed, that our entertainments were a   35
little more polite, or your taste a little less refined. But,
pray, madam, how came the poets and philosophers, that
laboured so much in hunting after pleasure, to place it at
last in a country life?

MRS. SULLEN

Because they wanted money, child, to find out the pleasures   40
of the town. Did you ever see a poet or philosopher worth
ten thousand pound? If you can show me such a man, I'll

29–30 *fat ale* strong, full-bodied ale
31 *plaisters* obsolete form of 'plasters'
   diet-drinks drinks prescribed and prepared for medicinal purposes
32 *stilling* distilling

19–20 *hospital child* a pauper in a charitable institution. According to their
   advocates, one prime function of such foundations was to 'teach the
   children of the poor . . . to know what their station in life is, how mean
   their circumstances, how necessary 'tis for them to be diligent, labor-
   ious, honest and faithful, humble and submissive, what duties they owe
   the rest of mankind and particularly to their superiors' (Isaac Watts,
   quoted in Asa Briggs (ed.), *How They Lived*: vol. III: *An Anthology of
   original documents written between 1700 and 1815* (Oxford, 1969), 343).
40 *Because they wanted money* Fitzgibbon aptly cites Farquhar's *The
   Recruiting Officer* (III.i): 'If he were not so well dressed, I should take
   him for a poet'.

lay you fifty pound you'll find him somewhere within the
weekly bills. Not that I disapprove rural pleasures, as the
poets have painted them; in their landscape, every Phyllis has   45
her Corydon, every murmuring stream, and every flowery
mead, gives fresh alarms to love. Besides, you'll find that
their couples were never married.—But yonder I see my
Corydon, and a sweet swain it is, Heaven knows! Come,
Dorinda, don't be angry; he's my husband, and your   50
brother: and, between both, is he not a sad brute?

DORINDA

I have nothing to say to your part of him—you're the best
judge.

MRS. SULLEN

O sister, sister! if ever you marry, beware of a sullen, silent
sot, one that's always musing, but never thinks. There's   55
some diversion in a talking blockhead; and since a woman
must wear chains, I would have the pleasure of hearing 'em
rattle a little. Now you shall see, but take this by the way:—
He came home this morning at his usual hour of four,
wakened me out of a sweet dream of something else, by   60
tumbling over the tea-table, which he broke all to pieces;
after his man and he had rolled about the room like sick
passengers in a storm, he comes flounce into bed, dead as a
salmon into a fishmonger's basket; his feet cold as ice, his
breath hot as a furnace, and his hands and his face as   65
greasy as his flannel nightcap.—O, matrimony!—He tosses
up the clothes with a barbarous swing over his shoulders,

43–4 *within the weekly bills* i.e., within London, for which city the weekly
  bills of mortality were issued.
45–6 *Phyllis . . . Corydon* common names for a shepherdess and shepherd
  in pastoral poetry.
49 *swain* a lover or wooer in pastoral poetry; but, also, a rustic or farm
  labourer, the latter meaning obviously fitting Mrs Sullen's uncom-
  plimentary opinion of her spouse.
56–7 *since a woman must wear chains* Mrs Sullen's assessment of the
  woman's lot in marriage is not mere exaggeration, but can be paralleled
  in many other contemporary accounts. Guy Miege, for example, informs his readers that 'by the Law of *England*, a Wife is so much in the
  Power of her Husband, that she can call nothing her own. And, when
  she offends,'tis in her Husband's Power to correct her, as a Servant'
  (*The New State of England, Under Our Present Monarch K. William III*
  (4th edition: London, 1702), Part II, 171). See also John
  Chamberlayne, *Magnae Britanniae Notitia* (London, 1708), p. 240.

disorders the whole economy of my bed, leaves me half
naked, and my whole night's comfort is the tuneable
serenade of that wakeful nightingale, his nose! O the   70
pleasure of counting the melancholy clock by a snoring
husband! But now, sister, you shall see how handsomely,
being a well-bred man, he will beg my pardon.

Enter SULLEN

SULLEN
My head aches consumedly.

MRS. SULLEN
Will you be pleased, my dear, to drink tea with us this   75
morning? It may do your head good.

SULLEN
No.

DORINDA
Coffee, brother?

SULLEN
Pshaw!

MRS. SULLEN
Will you please to dress and go to church with me? The air   80
may help you.

SULLEN
Scrub!

Enter SCRUB

SCRUB
Sir!

SULLEN
What day o'th' week is this?

SCRUB
Sunday, an't please your worship.   85

SULLEN
Sunday! bring me a dram, and d'ye hear, set out the
venison-pasty and a tankard of strong beer upon the hall-
table; I'll go to breakfast.   *Going*

DORINDA
Stay, stay, brother, you shan't get off so; you were very
naught last night, and must make your wife reparation;   90
come, come, brother, won't you ask pardon?

68 *economy* orderly arrangement
69 *tuneable* harmonious, tuneful
74 *consumedly* confoundedly
90 *naught* obsolete form of 'naughty', then a stronger term of
   rebuke than now

SULLEN
  For what?
DORINDA
  For being drunk last night.
SULLEN
  I can afford it, can't I?
MRS. SULLEN
  But I can't, sir.   95
SULLEN
  Then you may let it alone.
MRS. SULLEN
  But I must tell you, sir, that this is not to be borne.
SULLEN
  I'm glad on't.
MRS. SULLEN
  What is the reason, sir, that you use me thus inhumanly?
SULLEN
  Scrub!   100
SCRUB
  Sir!
SULLEN
  Get things ready to shave my head.   *Exit*
MRS. SULLEN
  Have a care of coming near his temples, Scrub, for fear you
  meet something there that may turn the edge of your razor.
  — [*Exit* SCRUB] Inveterate stupidity! Did you ever know so   105
  hard, so obstinate a spleen as his? O sister, sister! I shall
  never ha' good of the beast till I get him to town; London,
  dear London, is the place for managing and breaking a

102 *shave my head* so that his wig should fit tightly (Rothstein)
104 *something* i.e., the cuckold's horns
106 *spleen* ill-temper

---

107 ff. *London, dear London* This speech, and the two that follow, partly
    depend upon widespread contemporary assumptions about the greater
    licentiousness and moral freedom of life in London. For example, the
    sober demographer Gregory King even made arithmetical allowance for
    the 'more frequent Fornications and Adulteries' and the 'greater
    Luxury & Intemperance' in the capital in making statistical calculations
    concerning variations in birth-rate (*Two Tracts*, ed. G. E. Barnett
    (Baltimore, 1936), p. 28). For an example of a husband who agreed
    with Mrs Sullen and earnestly strove to compel his wife to 'be content
    to live to him in the country', see *Historical Manuscripts Commission
    Reports*, Rutland, vol. 2 (London, 1889), 31. But also relevant to the
    ladies' meditations is another aspect of London's contemporary repu-

husband.

DORINDA

And has not a husband the same opportunities there for   110
humbling a wife?

MRS. SULLEN

No, no, child, 'tis a standing maxim in conjugal discipline,
that when a man would enslave his wife, he hurries her
into the country; and when a lady would be arbitrary with
her husband, she wheedles her booby up to town. A man   115
dare not play the tyrant in London, because there are so
many examples to encourage the subject to rebel. O
Dorinda! Dorinda! a fine woman may do anything in
London: o'my conscience, she may raise an army of forty
thousand men.   120

DORINDA

I fancy, sister, you have a mind to be trying your power
that way here in Lichfield; you have drawn the French count
to your colours already.

MRS. SULLEN

The French are a people that can't live without their
gallantries.   125

DORINDA

And some English that I know, sister, are not averse to
such amusements.

---

tation. In referring to the husband as 'tyrant' and the wife as 'subject',
Mrs Sullen is invoking that traditional analogy between the roles of
king and husband which was still a formidable presence in all debates
on matrimonial issues. John Goodman, for example, could calmly
assert that 'every man being King in his own Family may give Laws to
it, and oblige those who are under his protection to pay him Allegiance'
(*The Old Religion Demonstrated in its Principles, and Described in the
Life and Practice thereof* (London, 1684), p. 253). The link between the
two kinds of authority was, in fact, still part of English criminal law; a
woman who slew her husband was guilty of petty treason, not murder,
and accordingly suffered a more savage penalty. In the seventeenth-
century political arena, London had a notably anti-royalist reputation—
based, in particular, upon the city's behaviour during the Civil War
and the Exclusion crisis. With the latter in mind, for example, Aphra
Behn could make one of her Whig characters gratefully remark: 'Come,
come, the World is not so bad yet, but a man may speak Treason
within the Walls of *London*, thanks be to God, and honest conscientious
Jury-men' (*The City Heiress* (London, 1682), p. 51). Thus, Mrs Sullen
can neatly argue that the history of the city's rebellious relationship
with the national monarch provides a pleasing precedent for a wife's
rebellion against that domestic monarch, a husband.

MRS. SULLEN

Well, sister, since the truth must out, it may do as well now
as hereafter; I think one way to rouse my lethargic, sottish
husband is to give him a rival: security begets negligence in all   130
people, and men must be alarmed to make 'em alert in
their duty. Women are like pictures, of no value in the
hands of a fool, till he hears men of sense bid high for the
purchase.

DORINDA

This might do, sister, if my brother's understanding were   135
to be convinced into a passion for you; but I fancy there's
a natural aversion of his side; and I fancy, sister, that you
don't come much behind him, if you dealt fairly.

MRS. SULLEN

I own it; we are united contradictions, fire and water. But I
could be contented, with a great many other wives, to   140
humour the censorious mob, and give the world an appearance of living well with my husband, could I bring him but
to dissemble a little kindness to keep me in countenance.

DORINDA

But how do you know, sister, but that, instead of rousing
your husband by this artifice to a counterfeit kindness, he   145
should awake in a real fury?

MRS. SULLEN

Let him; if I can't entice him to the one, I would provoke
him to the other.

DORINDA

But how must I behave myself between ye?

MRS. SULLEN

You must assist me.   150

DORINDA

What, against my own brother!

MRS. SULLEN

He's but half a brother, and I'm your entire friend. If I go a
step beyond the bounds of honour, leave me; till then, I
expect you should go along with me in everything; while I
trust my honour in your hands, you may trust your   155
brother's in mine.—The count is to dine here today.

DORINDA

'Tis a strange thing, sister, that I can't like that man.

MRS. SULLEN

You like nothing; your time is not come; love and death

141 *mob* the common people

have their fatalities, and strike home one time or other:
you'll pay for all one day, I warrant ye.—But, come, my   160
lady's tea is ready, and 'tis almost church-time.   *Exeunt*

[Act II, Scene ii]

Scene, the inn

Enter AIMWELL *dressed, and* ARCHER

AIMWELL
And was she the daughter of the house?
ARCHER
The landlord is so blind as to think so; but I dare swear she
has better blood in her veins.
AIMWELL
Why dost think so?
ARCHER
Because the baggage has a pert *je ne sais quoi*; she reads   5
plays, keeps a monkey, and is troubled with vapours.
AIMWELL
By which discoveries I guess that you know more of her.
ARCHER
Not yet, faith; the lady gives herself airs, forsooth, nothing
under a gentleman!
AIMWELL
Let me take her in hand.   10
ARCHER
Say one word more o'that, and I'll declare myself, spoil your
sport there, and everywhere else; look ye, Aimwell, every
man in his own sphere.
AIMWELL
Right; and therefore you must pimp for your master.
ARCHER
In the usual forms, good sir, after I have served myself.—But   15
to our business. You are so well dressed, Tom, and make so
handsome a figure, that I fancy you may do execution in a

5 *je ne sais quoi* an inexpressible quality
6 *vapours* a depression of spirits much cultivated by fashionable
ladies

6 *keeps a monkey* Cf. Rochester's description of the fine lady who
lavishes an extravagant display of affection upon her 'much esteemed
dear friend, the monkey' (in *A Letter from Artemisia in the Town to
Chloe in the Country*).

country church; the exterior part strikes first, and you're in
the right to make that impression favourable.

AIMWELL

There's something in that which may turn to advantage.   20
The appearance of a stranger in a country church draws as
many gazers as a blazing star; no sooner he comes into the
cathedral, but a train of whispers runs buzzing round the
congregation in a moment:—Who is he? Whence comes he?
Do you know him?—Then I, sir, tips me the verger with   25
half a crown; he pockets the simony, and inducts me into the
best pew in the church; I pull out my snuff-box, turn myself
round, bow to the bishop, or the dean, if he be the com-
manding officer; single out a beauty, rivet both my eyes to
hers, set my nose a-bleeding by the strength of imagination,   30
and show the whole church my concern by my endeavouring
to hide it; after the sermon, the whole town gives me to her
for a lover, and by persuading the lady that I am a-dying for
her, the tables are turned, and she in good earnest falls in
love with me.   35

ARCHER

There's nothing in this, Tom, without a precedent; but
instead of riveting your eyes to a beauty, try to fix 'em upon a
fortune; that's our business at present.

AIMWELL

Pshaw! no woman can be a beauty without a fortune. Let
me alone, for I am a marksman.   40

ARCHER

Tom!

AIMWELL

Ay.

ARCHER

When were you at church before, pray?

AIMWELL

Um—I was there at the coronation.

ARCHER

And how can you expect a blessing by going to church now?   45

AIMWELL

Blessing! nay, Frank, I ask but for a wife.   *Exit*

22 *blazing star* comet

---

26 *simony* the practice of buying or selling ecclesiastical offices; here
jokingly applied to Aimwell's purchase of 'the best pew'.
44 *coronation* Since the coronation of Queen Anne took place on 23 April
1702, Aimwell has not been in church for five years.

ARCHER
   Truly, the man is not very unreasonable in his demands.
                                 Exit at the opposite door

                  Enter BONIFACE *and* CHERRY
BONIFACE
   Well, daughter, as the saying is, have you brought Martin
   to confess?
CHERRY
   Pray, father, don't put me upon getting anything out of a   50
   man; I'm but young, you know, father, and I don't understand wheedling.
BONIFACE
   Young! why, you jade, as the saying is, can any woman
   wheedle that is not young? Your mother was useless at five
   and twenty. Not wheedle! would you make your mother a   55
   whore, and me a cuckold, as the saying is? I tell you, his
   silence confesses it, and his master spends his money so
   freely, and is so much a gentleman every manner of way,
   that he must be a highwayman.

                  Enter GIBBET *in a cloak*
GIBBET
   Landlord, landlord, is the coast clear?   60
BONIFACE
   O Mr. Gibbet, what's the news?
GIBBET
   No matter, ask no questions, all fair and honourable.—Here,
   my dear Cherry. (*Gives her a bag*) Two hundred sterling
   pounds, as good as any that ever hanged or saved a rogue;
   lay 'em by with the rest; and here—three wedding or mourn-   65
   ing rings, 'tis much the same, you know.—Here, two silver-
   hilted swords; I took those from fellows that never show
   any part of their swords but the hilts. Here is a diamond
   necklace which the lady hid in the privatest place in the
   coach, but I found it out. This gold watch I took from a   70
   pawnbroker's wife; it was left in her hands by a person of
   quality: there's the arms upon the case.
CHERRY
   But who had you the money from?

65–6 *mourning rings* rings worn in memory of the dead

47 s.d. *the opposite door* There were doors in the proscenium arch on either
   side of the stage in contemporary playhouses.

GIBBET

Ah! poor woman! I pitied her;—from a poor lady just
eloped from her husband. She had made up her cargo, and   75
was bound for Ireland as hard as she could drive; she
told me of her husband's barbarous usage, and so I left
her half a crown. But I had almost forgot, my dear Cherry;
I have a present for you.

CHERRY

What is't?   80

GIBBET

A pot of ceruse, my child, that I took out of a lady's under-
pocket.

CHERRY

What, Mr. Gibbet, do you think that I paint?

GIBBET

Why, you jade, your betters do; I'm sure the lady that I
took it from had a coronet upon her handkerchief.—Here,   85
take my cloak, and go, secure the premises.

CHERRY

I will secure 'em.   *Exit*

BONIFACE

But, hark ye, where's Hounslow and Bagshot?

GIBBET

They'll be here tonight.

BONIFACE

D'ye know of any other gentlemen o'the pad on this road?   90

GIBBET

No.

BONIFACE

I fancy that I have two that lodge in the house just now.

GIBBET

The devil! How d'ye smoke 'em?

BONIFACE

Why, the one is gone to church.

GIBBET

That's suspicious, I must confess.   95

BONIFACE

And the other is now in his master's chamber; he pretends

---

81 *ceruse* a white-lead cosmetic
83 *paint* use cosmetics
86 *premises* the articles previously mentioned
90 *gentlemen o'the pad* highwaymen
93 *smoke* get an inkling of, suspect

to be servant to the other; we'll call him out and pump him
a little.
GIBBET
With all my heart.
BONIFACE
Mr. Martin! Mr. Martin!   100

Enter ARCHER *combing a periwig and singing*

GIBBET
The roads are consumed deep; I'm as dirty as old Brentford
at Christmas.—A good pretty fellow that. Whose servant
are you, friend?
ARCHER
My master's.
GIBBET
Really?   105
ARCHER
Really.
GIBBET
That's much.—The fellow has been at the bar by his
evasions.—But, pray, sir, what is your master's name?
ARCHER
Tall, all, dall!—(*Sings and combs the periwig*) This is the
most obstinate curl—   110
GIBBET
I ask you his name?
ARCHER
Name, sir—*tall, all, dall!*—I never asked him his name in
my life.—*Tall, all, dall!*
BONIFACE
What think you now?
GIBBET
Plain, plain; he talks now as if he were before a judge.—But, 115
pray, friend, which way does your master travel?
ARCHER
A-horseback.
GIBBET
Very well again, an old offender, right.—But, I mean, does
he go upwards or downwards?

100 s.d. *Enter* ARCHER ed. (*Enter* Martin Q)

---

101 *Brentford* a town to the west of London—its unsavoury reputation can
be gauged from James Thomson's description of it as 'a town of mud'
(*The Castle of Indolence*, Canto II, Stanza lxxxi).

ARCHER

Downwards, I fear, sir.—*Tall, all*!   120

GIBBET

I'm afraid my fate will be a contrary way.

BONIFACE

Ha! ha! ha! Mr. Martin, you're very arch. This gentleman
is only travelling towards Chester, and would be glad of
your company, that's all.—Come, captain, you'll stay
tonight, I suppose; I'll show you a chamber—come,   125
captain.   [*Exit*]

GIBBET

Farewell, friend!   *Exit*

ARCHER

Captain, your servant.—Captain! a pretty fellow! 'Sdeath, I
wonder that the officers of the army don't conspire to beat
all scoundrels in red but their own.   130

Enter CHERRY

CHERRY

(*Aside*) Gone, and Martin here! I hope he did not listen; I
would have the merit of the discovery all my own, because
I would oblige him to love me.—Mr. Martin, who was that
man with my father?

ARCHER

Some recruiting sergeant, or whipped-out trooper, I suppose.   135

CHERRY

All's safe, I find.

ARCHER

Come, my dear, have you conned over the catechise I
taught you last night?

CHERRY

Come, question me.

ARCHER

What is love?   140

CHERRY

Love is I know not what, it comes I know not how, and
goes I know not when.

---

121 *a contrary way* i.e., he is destined to mount the gallows

135 *whipped-out trooper* For some offences, a soldier's dismissal from the
     army was accompanied by a flogging.
137 *catechise* catechism; part of the following dialogue, with other extracts
     from the play, was printed separately in *Love's Catechism* (1707)—see
     Stonehill, II, 347–50.

ARCHER
Very well, an apt scholar.—(*Chucks her under the chin*)
Where does love enter?

CHERRY
Into the eyes.   145

ARCHER
And where go out?

CHERRY
I won't tell ye.

ARCHER
What are objects of that passion?

CHERRY
Youth, beauty, and clean linen.

ARCHER
The reason?   150

CHERRY
The two first are fashionable in nature, and the third at
court.

ARCHER
That's my dear.—What are the signs and tokens of that
passion?

CHERRY
A stealing look, a stammering tongue, words improbable, de-   155
signs impossible, and actions impracticable.

ARCHER
That's my good child! Kiss me.—What must a lover do to
obtain his mistress?

CHERRY
He must adore the person that disdains him, he must bribe
the chambermaid that betrays him, and court the footman   160
that laughs at him. He must—he must—

ARCHER
Nay, child, I must whip you if you don't mind your lesson;
he must treat his—

CHERRY
O, ay!—He must treat his enemies with respect, his friends
with indifference, and all the world with contempt; he must   165
suffer much, and fear more; he must desire much, and hope
little; in short, he must embrace his ruin, and throw himself
away.

ARCHER
Had ever man so hopeful a pupil as mine?—Come, my dear,
why is love called a riddle?   170

CHERRY

Because, being blind, he leads those that see, and, though a
child, he governs a man.

ARCHER

Mighty well!—And why is love pictured blind?

CHERRY

Because the painters, out of the weakness or privilege of
their art, chose to hide those eyes that they could not draw.   175

ARCHER

That's my dear little scholar; kiss me again.—And why
should love, that's a child, govern a man?

CHERRY

Because that a child is the end of love.

ARCHER

And so ends love's catechism.—And now, my dear, we'll
go in, and make my master's bed.   180

CHERRY

Hold, hold, Mr. Martin! You have taken a great deal of
pains to instruct me, and what d'ye think I have learned by
it?

ARCHER

What?

CHERRY

That your discourse and your habit are contradictions, and   185
it would be nonsense in me to believe you a footman any
longer.

ARCHER

'Oons, what a witch it is!

CHERRY

Depend upon this, sir: nothing in this garb shall ever
tempt me; for, though I was born to servitude, I hate it.   190
Own your condition, swear you love me, and then—

ARCHER

And then we shall go make the bed?

CHERRY

Yes.

ARCHER

You must know then, that I am born a gentleman; my
education was liberal: but I went to London a younger   195
brother, fell into the hands of sharpers, who stripped me of

188 *'Oons* an oath, a contraction of 'By God's wounds'
191 *condition* social position, rank
196 *sharpers* swindlers, rogues

my money; my friends disowned me, and now my necessity
brings me to what you see.

CHERRY

Then take my hand—promise to marry me before you
sleep, and I'll make you master of two thousand pound.   200

ARCHER

How?

CHERRY

Two thousand pound that I have this minute in my own
custody; so throw off your livery this instant, and I'll go find
a parson.

ARCHER

What said you? A parson!   205

CHERRY

What! Do you scruple?

ARCHER

Scruple! no, no, but—two thousand pound, you say?

CHERRY

And better.

ARCHER

'Sdeath, what shall I do?—But hark'ee, child, what need
you make me master of yourself and money, when you may   210
have the same pleasure out of me, and still keep your
fortune in your hands?

CHERRY

Then you won't marry me?

ARCHER

I would marry you, but—

CHERRY

O sweet sir, I'm your humble servant; you're fairly caught!   215
Would you persuade me that any gentleman who could bear
the scandal of wearing a livery would refuse two thousand
pound, let the condition be what it would? No, no, sir.—But
I hope you'll pardon the freedom I have taken, since it was
only to inform myself of the respect that I ought to pay you.   220
                                                                                        Going

ARCHER

Fairly bit, by Jupiter!—Hold! hold!—And have you
actually two thousand pound?

CHERRY

Sir, I have my secrets as well as you; when you please to be
more open, I shall be more free, and be assured that I have

221 *bit* taken in, tricked

discoveries that will match yours, be what they will. In the   225
meanwhile, be satisfied that no discovery I make shall ever
hurt you, but beware of my father!   [*Exit*]

ARCHER

So! we're like to have as many adventures in our inn as
Don Quixote had in his. Let me see—two thousand pound!
—If the wench would promise to die when the money were   230
spent, egad, one would marry her; but the fortune may
go off in a year or two, and the wife may live—Lord knows
how long! Then, an innkeeper's daughter! ay, that's the
devil—there my pride brings me off.

>For whatsoe'er the sages charge on pride,   235
>The angels' fall, and twenty faults beside,
>On earth, I'm sure, 'mong us of mortal calling,
>Pride saves man oft, and woman too, from falling.   *Exit*

Act III, [Scene i]

[*Scene*, LADY BOUNTIFUL's *house*]
Enter MRS. SULLEN [*and*] DORINDA

MRS. SULLEN

Ha! ha! ha! my dear sister, let me embrace thee! Now we
are friends indeed; for I shall have a secret of yours as a
pledge for mine. Now you'll be good for something; I shall
have you conversable in the subjects of the sex.

DORINDA

But do you think that I am so weak as to fall in love with a   5
fellow at first sight?

MRS. SULLEN

Pshaw! now you spoil all; why should not we be as free in our

---

238 s.d. *Exit* Q follows this with '*End of the Second Act*'
s.d. *Scene*, LADY BOUNTIFUL's *house* ed. (SCENE *continues* Q)
   4 *conversable* able or disposed to talk

---

229 *Don Quixote* Cervantes's novel was both popular and influential during
   this period. Three plays dramatizing Don Quixote's adventures, including those in the inn, were offered to London audiences by Thomas
   D'Urfey in 1694–95; in 1707, the first two of these (compressed into a
   single play) were still regular items in the playhouse repertoire. The
   appearance of material from *Don Quixote* on the English stage during
   these years is chronicled by Gordon K. Thomas, 'The Knight amid the
   Dunces', *Restoration and Eighteenth-Century Theatre Research*, vol. 14
   (1975), 10–22.

friendships as the men? I warrant you, the gentleman has
got to his confidant already, has avowed his passion, toasted
your health, called you ten thousand angels, has run over   10
your lips, eyes, neck, shape, air, and everything, in a
description that warms their mirth to a second enjoyment.

DORINDA

Your hand, sister, I an't well.

MRS. SULLEN

So—she's breeding already.—Come, child, up with it—hem
a little—so—now tell me, don't you like the gentleman that   15
we saw at church just now?

DORINDA

The man's well enough.

MRS. SULLEN

Well enough! Is he not a demigod, a Narcissus, a star, the
man i'the moon?

DORINDA

O sister, I'm extremely ill!   20

MRS. SULLEN

Shall I send to your mother, child, for a little of her cephalic
plaister to put to the soles of your feet, or shall I send to the
gentleman for something for you? Come, unlace your stays,
unbosom yourself. The man is perfectly a pretty fellow, I
saw him when he first came into church.   25

DORINDA

I saw him too, sister, and with an air that shone, methought,
like rays about his person.

MRS. SULLEN

Well said: up with it!

DORINDA

No forward coquette behaviour, no airs to set him off, no
studied looks nor artful posture—but nature did it all—   30

MRS. SULLEN

Better and better!—one touch more—come!

DORINDA

But then his looks—did you observe his eyes?

MRS. SULLEN

Yes, yes, I did.—His eyes, well, what of his eyes?

DORINDA

Sprightly, but not wandering, they seemed to view, but

21–2 *cephalic plaister* a plaster for relieving disorders of the head; 'Mrs.
Sullen is suggesting that Dorinda has been turned topsy-turvy'
(Rothstein).

never gazed on anything but me.—And then his looks so   35
humble were, and yet so noble, that they aimed to tell me
that he could with pride die at my feet, though he scorned
slavery anywhere else.

MRS. SULLEN

The physic works purely.—How d'ye find yourself now, my
dear?   40

DORINDA

Hem! much better, my dear.—O, here comes our Mercury!

Enter SCRUB

Well, Scrub, what news of the gentleman?

SCRUB

Madam, I have brought you a packet of news.

DORINDA

Open it quickly, come.

SCRUB

In the first place I inquired who the gentleman was; they   45
told me, he was a stranger. Secondly, I asked what the
gentleman was; they answered and said, that they never
saw him before. Thirdly, I inquired what countryman he
was; they replied, 'twas more than they knew. Fourthly, I
demanded whence he came; their answer was, they could   50
not tell. And, fifthly, I asked whither he went, and they
replied, they knew nothing of the matter—and this is all I
could learn.

MRS. SULLEN

But what do the people say? Can't they guess?

SCRUB

Why, some think he's a spy, some guess he's a mounte-   55
bank; some say one thing, some another: but, for my own
part, I believe he's a Jesuit.

DORINDA

A Jesuit! Why a Jesuit?

SCRUB

Because he keeps his horses always ready saddled, and his
footman talks French.   60

MRS. SULLEN

His footman!

39 *physic* medicine
39 *purely* excellently
41 *Mercury* the messenger of the gods
55–6 *mountebank* itinerant quack

SCRUB

Ay, he and the count's footman were gabbering French like
two intriguing ducks in a mill-pond; and I believe they
talked of me, for they laughed consumedly.

DORINDA

What sort of livery has the footman?   65

SCRUB

Livery! Lord, madam, I took him for a captain, he's so
bedizened with lace. And then he has tops to his shoes,
up to his mid leg, a silver-headed cane dangling at his
knuckles; he carries his hands in his pockets just so—
(*Walks in the French air*) —and has a fine long periwig tied   70
up in a bag.— Lord, madam, he's clear another sort of man
than I!

MRS. SULLEN

That may easily be.—But what shall we do now, sister?

DORINDA

I have it.—This fellow has a world of simplicity, and some
cunning; the first hides the latter by abundance.—Scrub!   75

SCRUB

Madam!

DORINDA

We have a great mind to know who this gentleman is, only
for our satisfaction.

SCRUB

Yes, madam, it would be a satisfaction, no doubt.

DORINDA

You must go and get acquainted with his footman, and   80
invite him hither to drink a bottle of your ale, because you're
butler today.

SCRUB

Yes, madam, I am butler every Sunday.

MRS. SULLEN

O brave! sister, o' my conscience, you understand the

62 *gabbering* talking volubly, jabbering
67 *tops* uppermost part of the leg of a high-boot or riding-boot
71 *bag* small silken pouch to contain the back-hair of a wig

---

70 s.d. *the French air* Remarks on the formidable influence of the latest
French fashions upon English gentlemen are frequent in post-1660
comedies. In Thomas Shadwell's *A True Widow* (I.i), for example,
Stanmore describes 'a gentleman who was so ugly a modish spark
would scarce give him a livery; yet by a correspondence he kept with a
tailor and shoemaker in Paris, and two or three of that sort, got one of
the finest women in England'.

mathematics already. 'Tis the best plot in the world: your   85
mother, you know, will be gone to church, my spouse will
be got to the alehouse with his scoundrels, and the house
will be our own—so we drop in by accident and ask the
fellow some questions ourselves. In the country, you know,
any stranger is company, and we're glad to take up with the   90
butler in a country dance, and happy if he'll do us the
favour.

SCRUB

O madam, you wrong me! I never refused your ladyship the
favour in my life.

Enter GIPSY

GIPSY

Ladies, dinner's upon table.   95

DORINDA

Scrub, we'll excuse your waiting—go where we ordered you.

SCRUB

I shall.   *Exeunt*

[Act III, Scene ii]

Scene changes to the inn
Enter AIMWELL *and* ARCHER

ARCHER

Well, Tom, I find you're a marksman.

AIMWELL

A marksman! who so blind could be, as not discern a swan
among the ravens?

ARCHER

Well, but hark'ee, Aimwell!

AIMWELL

Aimwell! call me Oroondates, Cesario, Amadis, all that   5

87 *scoundrels* a mean rascal, a low petty villain (Dr Johnson's
Dictionary)

---

94 *favour* Scrub, presumably deliberately, misunderstands his mistress's
remark as a reference to what the period frequently called 'the last
favour'.

5 *Oroondates* a character in La Calprenède's romance *Cassandra*; there
had also been a Restoration play by John Banks, *The Rival Kings, or, The
Loves of Oroondates and Statira* (first performed in 1677).

5 *Cesario* presumably a reference to the name adopted by the disguised
Viola in Shakespeare's *Twelfth Night*, although this play was not particularly well known or popular during the period.

5 *Amadis* Amadis de Gaul, the hero of a very popular prose romance, the
earliest surviving version of which is in Spanish.

romance can in a lover paint, and then I'll answer. O
Archer! I read her thousands in her looks; she looked like
Ceres in her harvest: corn, wine and oil, milk and honey,
gardens, groves, and purling streams played on her plenteous
face.   10

ARCHER

Her face! her pocket, you mean; the corn, wine, and oil
lies there. In short, she has ten thousand pound; that's the
English on't.

AIMWELL

Her eyes—

ARCHER

Are demi-cannons, to be sure; so I won't stand their   15
battery.   *Going*

AIMWELL

Pray excuse me, my passion must have vent.

ARCHER

Passion! what a plague! D'ye think these romantic airs will
do our business? Were my temper as extravagant as yours,
my adventures have something more romantic by half.   20

AIMWELL

Your adventures!

ARCHER

Yes,

> The nymph that with her twice ten hundred pounds,
> With brazen engine hot, and coif clear-starched,
> Can fire the guest in warming of the bed—   25

There's a touch of sublime Milton for you, and the subject
but an innkeeper's daughter! I can play with a girl as an
angler does with his fish; he keeps it at the end of his line,
runs it up the stream, and down the stream, till at last he
brings it to hand, tickles the trout, and so whips it into his   30
basket.

Enter BONIFACE

15 *demi-cannons* a large gun (of about 6½ inches bore)
24 *brazen engine* warming pan
24 *coif* a close-fitting cap
24 *clear-starched* stiffened with colourless starch

26 *sublime Milton* Archer is here essaying a contribution to a current vogue
   (of the 1690s and early 1700s) for writing Miltonic burlesque. The
   most popular work of this kind was Ambrose Philips's *The Splendid
   Shilling* (first published anonymously in 1701); by 1720 it had been
   reprinted nine times (both by itself and in miscellanies).

BONIFACE

Mr. Martin, as the saying is—yonder's an honest fellow
below, my Lady Bountiful's butler, who begs the honour
that you would go home with him and see his cellar.

ARCHER

Do my *baisemains* to the gentleman, and tell him I will do   35
myself the honour to wait on him immediately.

                                        Exit BONIFACE

AIMWELL

What do I hear?
            Soft Orpheus play, and fair Toftida sing!

ARCHER

Pshaw! damn your raptures! I tell you, here's a pump going
to be put into the vessel, and the ship will get into harbour,   40
my life on't. You say there's another lady, very handsome,
there?

AIMWELL

Yes, faith.

ARCHER

I am in love with her already.

AIMWELL

Can't you give me a bill upon Cherry in the meantime?   45

ARCHER

No, no, friend, all her corn, wine, and oil is engrossed to my
market. And once more I warn you to keep your anchorage
clear of mine; for if you fall foul of me, by this light you
shall go to the bottom! What! make prize of my little frigate,
while I am upon the cruise for you!—   *Exit*   50

                  Enter BONIFACE

AIMWELL

Well, well, I won't.—Landlord, have you any tolerable
company in the house? I don't care for dining alone.

BONIFACE

Yes, sir, there's a captain below, as the saying is, that
arrived about an hour ago.

AIMWELL

Gentlemen of his coat are welcome everywhere; will you   55

35 *baisemains* literally, a kiss of the hands; respects, compliments
46 *engrossed* monopolized, bought up
49 *frigate* a light, swift vessel

38 *Toftida* Mrs Katherine Tofts, the celebrated singer; the Drury Lane
   company offered her talents as the competing attraction to the first
   performance of *The Beaux' Stratagem.*

make him a compliment from me, and tell him I should be glad of his company?

BONIFACE

Who shall I tell him, sir, would—

AIMWELL

[*Aside*] Ha! that stroke was well thrown in!—I'm only a traveller like himself, and would be glad of his company, that's all. 60

BONIFACE

I obey your commands, as the saying is. *Exit*

Enter ARCHER

ARCHER

'Sdeath! I had forgot; what title will you give yourself?

AIMWELL

My brother's, to be sure; he would never give me anything else, so I'll make bold with his honour this bout:—you know the rest of your cue. 65

ARCHER

Ay, ay. [*Exit*]

Enter GIBBET

GIBBET

Sir, I'm yours.

AIMWELL

'Tis more than I deserve, sir, for I don't know you.

GIBBET

I don't wonder at that, sir, for you never saw me before— (*Aside*) I hope. 70

AIMWELL

And pray, sir, how came I by the honour of seeing you now?

GIBBET

Sir, I scorn to intrude upon any gentleman—but my landlord—

AIMWELL

O sir, I ask your pardon; you're the captain he told me of? 75

GIBBET

At your service, sir.

AIMWELL

What regiment, may I be so bold?

GIBBET

A marching regiment, sir, an old corps.

67 s.d. [*Exit*] ed. (*Exit* Bon. Q)

AIMWELL

(*Aside*) Very old, if your coat be regimental.—You have
served abroad, sir?   80

GIBBET

Yes, sir, in the plantations; 'twas my lot to be sent into the
worst service; I would have quitted it indeed, but a man of
honour, you know—Besides, 'twas for the good of my
country that I should be abroad:—anything for the good of
one's country—I'm a Roman for that.   85

AIMWELL

(*Aside*) One of the first, I'll lay my life.—You found the
West Indies very hot, sir?

GIBBET

Ay, sir, too hot for me.

AIMWELL

Pray, sir, han't I seen your face at Will's coffee-house?

GIBBET

Yes, sir, and at White's too.   90

AIMWELL

And where is your company now, captain?

GIBBET

They an't come yet.

AIMWELL

Why, d'ye expect 'em here?

---

81 *in the plantations* The implication of this, and of what follows, is that
   Gibbet had not gone abroad as a soldier, but had been transported to
   the plantations as a convicted criminal. However, he has not chosen a
   particularly salubrious disguise; the regiments serving in the West
   Indies were especially notorious for appalling discipline and morale—
   see Major R. E. Scouller, *The Armies of Queen Anne* (London, 1966),
   p. 292.

85 *Roman* in military terminology, a foot soldier who gave his pay to his
   captain to be allowed to serve and thus, like an ancient Roman, served
   only for honour and the love of his country.

86 *One of the first* Strauss suggested that the allusion here was 'to the
   character of the rabble that, in legendary history, responded to the offer
   by Romulus of a refuge to all in his new city of Rome'.

89 *Will's coffee-house* a famous London establishment, which was nick-
   named 'the Wits Coffee-House' (see, for example, William Wycherley,
   Works, ed. Montague Summers (London, 1924), vol. 2, 201). It
   numbered Dryden and Congreve among its distinguished clients.

90 *White's* a fashionable London chocolate-house. Swift and Steele were
   among those who frequented it.

GIBBET

They'll be here tonight, sir.

AIMWELL

Which way do they march?   95

GIBBET

Across the country.—[*Aside*] The devil's in't, if I han't said
enough to encourage him to declare! But I'm afraid he's not
right; I must tack about.

AIMWELL

Is your company to quarter in Lichfield?

GIBBET

In this house, sir.   100

AIMWELL

What! all?

GIBBET

My company's but thin, ha! ha! ha! We are but three, ha!
ha! ha!

AIMWELL

You're merry, sir.

GIBBET

Ay, sir, you must excuse me, sir; I understand the world,   105
especially the art of travelling: I don't care, sir, for answer-
ing questions directly upon the road—for I generally ride
with a charge about me.

AIMWELL (*Aside*)

Three or four, I believe.

GIBBET

I am credibly informed that there are highwaymen upon   110
this quarter; not, sir, that I could suspect a gentleman of
your figure—but truly, sir, I have got such a way of evasion
upon the road, that I don't care for speaking truth to any
man.

AIMWELL

Your caution may be necessary.—Then I presume you're no   115
captain?

GIBBET

Not I, sir; captain is a good travelling name, and so I take
it; it stops a great many foolish inquiries that are generally

---

98 *tack about* proceed obliquely by another course

108–9 *charge* Gibbet uses 'charge' to mean 'a sum of money', but Aimwell
uses it in the sense of 'a load of powder and shot for a firearm'.

made about gentlemen that travel; it gives a man an air of
something, and makes the drawers obedient:—and thus far   120
I am a captain, and no farther.

AIMWELL

And pray, sir, what is your true profession?

GIBBET

O sir, you must excuse me!—upon my word, sir, I don't
think it safe to tell you.

AIMWELL

Ha! ha! ha! upon my word, I commend you.   125

Enter BONIFACE

Well, Mr. Boniface, what's the news?

BONIFACE

There's another gentleman below, as the saying is, that,
hearing you were but two, would be glad to make the third
man, if you would give him leave.

AIMWELL

What is he?   130

BONIFACE

A clergyman, as the saying is.

AIMWELL

A clergyman! Is he really a clergyman? or is it only his
travelling name, as my friend the captain has it?

BONIFACE

O sir, he's a priest and chaplain to the French officers in
town.   135

AIMWELL

Is he a Frenchman?

BONIFACE

Yes, sir, born at Brussels.

GIBBET

A Frenchman, and a priest! I won't be seen in his company,
sir; I have a value for my reputation, sir.

AIMWELL

Nay, but, captain, since we are by ourselves—Can he speak 140
English, landlord?

BONIFACE

Very well, sir; you may know him, as the saying is, to be a
foreigner by his accent, and that's all.

120 *drawers* of ale; waiters at an inn

AIMWELL
Then he has been in England before?
BONIFACE
Never, sir; but he's a master of languages, as the saying is;   145
he talks Latin—it does me good to hear him talk Latin.
AIMWELL
Then you understand Latin, Mr. Boniface?
BONIFACE
Not I, sir, as the saying is; but he talks it so very fast, that
I'm sure it must be good.
AIMWELL
Pray, desire him to walk up.   150
BONIFACE
Here he is, as the saying is.

Enter FOIGARD

FOIGARD
Save you, gentlemens, both.
AIMWELL
A Frenchman!—Sir, your most humble servant.
FOIGARD
Och, dear joy, I am your most faithful shervant, and yours
alsho.   155
GIBBET
Doctor, you talk very good English, but you have a mighty
twang of the foreigner.
FOIGARD
My English is very vel for the vords, but we foreigners, you
know, cannot bring our tongues about the pronunciation
so soon.   160
AIMWELL
(*Aside*) A foreigner! a downright Teague, by this light!—
Were you born in France, doctor?

154 *dear joy* frequently used in late seventeenth- and early eighteenth-
     century drama as a characteristically Irish expression.
161 *downright Teague* pure Irish. 'Teague' was a common nickname for an
     Irishman in the seventeenth and eighteenth centuries; Farquhar (him-
     self, of course, Irish) dubs the Irish servant Teague in *The Twin Rivals*.
     Some earlier dramatic uses of the name are examined by Florence R.
     Scott, 'Teg—The Stage Irishman', *Modern Language Review*, vol. XLII
     (1947), 314–20.

FOIGARD

I was educated in France, but I was borned at Brussels; I
am a subject of the King of Spain, joy.

GIBBET

What King of Spain, sir? speak!   165

FOIGARD

Upon my shoul, joy, I cannot tell you as yet.

AIMWELL

Nay, captain, that was too hard upon the doctor; he's a
stranger.

FOIGARD

O, let him alone, dear joy; I am of a nation that is not easily
put out of countenance.   170

AIMWELL

Come, gentlemen, I'll end the dispute.—Here, landlord, is
dinner ready?

BONIFACE

Upon the table, as the saying is.

AIMWELL

Gentlemen—pray—that door—

FOIGARD

No, no, fait, the captain must lead.   175

AIMWELL

No, doctor, the church is our guide.

GIBBET

Ay, ay, so it is.   *Exit foremost, they follow*

---

163 *Brussels* Farquhar has been careful in his choice of an alleged birthplace
   for Foigard. Brussels (part of the Spanish Netherlands) had been an
   object of unsuccessful French aggression in the 1690s. When Charles II
   of Spain died in 1700, the Spanish governor of the city proclaimed his
   allegiance to Philip, and consequently (see following note), in the early
   years of the War of the Spanish Succession, the town was very firmly
   within the French sphere of influence. After Marlborough's major
   victory at Ramillies in 1706, however, Brussels fell to the Allies. Thus,
   Foigard, a chaplain in the service of the French, is in the unhappy
   position of coming (or so he claims) from a town which the French have
   recently, and in fairly disastrous circumstances, been forced to aban-
   don.

165 *What King of Spain* In 1707, with the War of the Spanish Succession
   still in progress, it remained in doubt whether Philip, the grandson of
   Louis XIV, or the Archduke Charles of Austria would become king of
   Spain. Foigard, a French sympathizer, would naturally support the
   claim of Philip, while English military and naval strength was being
   used on behalf of Charles.

[Act III, Scene iii]

Scene changes to a gallery in LADY BOUNTIFUL'*s house*
Enter ARCHER *and* SCRUB *singing, and hugging one another,*
SCRUB *with a tankard in his hand*—GIPSY *listening at a distance*

SCRUB

Tall, all, dall!—Come, my dear boy, let's have that song
once more.

ARCHER

No, no, we shall disturb the family.—But will you be sure
to keep the secret?

SCRUB

Pho! upon my honour, as I'm a gentleman.   5

ARCHER

'Tis enough. You must know, then, that my master is the
Lord Viscount Aimwell; he fought a duel t'other day in
London, wounded his man so dangerously, that he thinks
fit to withdraw till he hears whether the gentleman's
wounds be mortal or not. He never was in this part of   10
England before, so he chose to retire to this place, that's all.

GIPSY

And that's enough for me.   *Exit*

SCRUB

And where were you when your master fought?

ARCHER

We never know of our masters' quarrels.

SCRUB

No! If our masters in the country here receive a challenge, 15
the first thing they do is to tell their wives; the wife tells the
servants, the servants alarm the tenants, and in half an hour
you shall have the whole county in arms.

ARCHER

To hinder two men from doing what they have no mind for.
—But if you should chance to talk now of my business?   20

SCRUB

Talk! ay, sir, had I not learned the knack of holding my
tongue, I had never lived so long in a great family.

ARCHER

Ay, ay, to be sure, there are secrets in all families.

SCRUB

Secrets! ay; but I'll say no more. Come, sit down, we'll
make an end of our tankard: here—   25

ARCHER

With all my heart; who knows but you and I may come to
be better acquainted, eh? Here's your ladies' healths; you
have three, I think, and to be sure there must be secrets
among 'em.

SCRUB

Secrets! Ay, friend; I wish I had a friend—   30

ARCHER

Am not I your friend? Come, you and I will be sworn
brothers.

SCRUB

Shall we?

ARCHER

From this minute. Give me a kiss:—and now, brother Scrub.

SCRUB

And now, brother Martin, I will tell you a secret that will   35
make your hair stand on end. You must know that I am
consumedly in love.

ARCHER

That's a terrible secret, that's the truth on't.

SCRUB

That jade, Gipsy, that was with us just now in the cellar, is
the arrantest whore that ever wore a petticoat; and I'm dying   40
for love of her.

ARCHER

Ha! ha! ha!—Are you in love with her person or her virtue,
brother Scrub?

SCRUB

I should like virtue best, because it is more durable than
beauty; for virtue holds good with some women long, and   45
many a day after they have lost it.

ARCHER

In the country, I grant ye, where no woman's virtue is lost,
till a bastard be found.

SCRUB

Ay, could I bring her to a bastard, I should have her all to
myself; but I dare not put it upon that lay, for fear of being   50
sent for a soldier. Pray, brother, how do you gentlemen in
London like that same Pressing Act?

50 *put it upon that lay* take that line

---

52 *Pressing Act* As a result of chronic shortages of manpower for the army,
a series of Acts, beginning in the parliamentary session of 1703–04,
empowered Justices of the Peace 'to raise and levy such able-bodied

ARCHER

Very ill, brother Scrub; 'tis the worst that ever was made for us. Formerly I remember the good days, when we could dun our masters for our wages, and if they refused to pay us, 55 we could have a warrant to carry 'em before a justice; but now if we talk of eating, they have a warrant for us, and carry us before three justices.

SCRUB

And to be sure we go, if we talk of eating; for the justices won't give their own servants a bad example. Now this is 60 my misfortune—I dare not speak in the house, while that jade Gipsy dings about like a fury.—Once I had the better end of the staff.

ARCHER

And how comes the change now?

SCRUB

Why, the mother of all this mischief is a priest. 65

ARCHER

A priest!

SCRUB

Ay, a damned son of a whore of Babylon, that came over hither to say grace to the French officers, and eat up our provisions.—There's not a day goes over his head without dinner or supper in this house. 70

ARCHER

How came he so familiar in the family?

---

54 *dun* importune for money due
62 *dings* flings
62–3 *the better end of the staff* the advantage
67 *whore of Babylon* the Church of Rome; a characteristically seventeenth-century Protestant interpretation of Revelation 17, 18

---

men as have not any lawful calling or employment, or visible means for their maintenance and livelihood, to serve as soldiers'. Courts of three justices sat to decide who was liable to impressment; for the operation of one such, see *The Recruiting Officer* (V.v). For the campaigning season of 1708, surviving records inform us that Scrub's county, Staffordshire, yielded twenty volunteers and twenty-eight impressed men (Scouller, op. cit., p. 374).

71 *so familiar in the family* Cf. Samuel Butler on the character of a popish priest: 'He never gets within a Family, but he gets on the Top of it, and governs all down to the Bottom of the Cellar' (*Characters*, ed. Charles W. Daves (London and Cleveland, 1970), p. 100).

SCRUB

Because he speaks English as if he had lived here all his life, and tells lies as if he had been a traveller from his cradle.

ARCHER

And this priest, I'm afraid, has converted the affections of your Gipsy.   75

SCRUB

Converted! ay, and perverted, my dear friend: for, I'm afraid, he has made her a whore and a papist. But this is not all; there's the French count and Mrs. Sullen, they're in the confederacy, and for some private ends of their own, to be sure.   80

ARCHER

A very hopeful family yours, brother Scrub! I suppose the maiden lady has her lover too?

SCRUB

Not that I know: she's the best on 'em, that's the truth on't. But they take care to prevent my curiosity, by giving me so much business, that I'm a perfect slave. What d'ye think is   85
my place in this family?

ARCHER

Butler, I suppose.

SCRUB

Ah, Lord help you! I'll tell you. Of a Monday I drive the coach, of a Tuesday I drive the plough, on Wednesday I follow the hounds, a Thursday I dun the tenants, on Friday   90
I go to market, on Saturday I draw warrants, and a Sunday I draw beer.

ARCHER

Ha! ha! ha! if variety be a pleasure in life, you have enough on't, my dear brother. But what ladies are those?

[SCRUB]

Ours, ours; that upon the right hand is Mrs. Sullen, and the   95
other is Mrs. Dorinda. Don't mind 'em; sit still, man.

Enter MRS. SULLEN *and* DORINDA

95 s.p. SCRUB ed. (*Arch.* Q)

73 *a traveller* a common prejudice—cf. Sir Thomas Overbury's character of an 'Affectate Traveller', who 'chuseth rather to tell lies, then not wonders' (*Miscellaneous Works*, ed. Edward F. Rimbault (London, 1890), p. 59).

91 *draw warrants* his master, Squire Sullen, being, of course, a justice of the peace.

MRS. SULLEN

I have heard my brother talk of my Lord Aimwell, but they
say that his brother is the finer gentleman.

DORINDA

That's impossible, sister.

MRS. SULLEN

He's vastly rich, but very close, they say.   100

DORINDA

No matter for that; if I can creep into his heart, I'll open
his breast, I warrant him: I have heard say, that people may
be guessed at by the behaviour of their servants; I could
wish we might talk to that fellow.

MRS. SULLEN

So do I; for I think he's a very pretty fellow. Come this   105
way, I'll throw out a lure for him presently.

    They walk a turn towards the opposite side of the stage; MRS.
    SULLEN *drops her glove,* ARCHER *runs, takes it up, and gives*
    it to her

ARCHER

Corn, wine, and oil, indeed!—But, I think, the wife has the
greatest plenty of flesh and blood; she should be my choice.
—Ah, a, say you so!—Madam—your ladyship's glove.

MRS. SULLEN

O sir, I thank you!—What a handsome bow the fellow has!   110

DORINDA

Bow! Why, I have known several footmen come down
from London set up here for dancing-masters, and carry
off the best fortunes in the country.

ARCHER

(*Aside*) That project, for aught I know, had been better
than ours.—Brother Scrub, why don't you introduce me?   115

SCRUB

Ladies, this is the strange gentleman's servant that you see
at church today; I understood he came from London, and
so I invited him to the cellar, that he might show me the
newest flourish in whetting my knives.

DORINDA

And I hope you have made much of him?   120

ARCHER

O yes, madam, but the strength of your ladyship's liquor is
a little too potent for the constitution of your humble
servant.

MRS. SULLEN

What, then you don't usually drink ale?

ARCHER

No, madam; my constant drink is tea, or a little wine and   125
water. 'Tis prescribed me by the physician for a remedy
against the spleen.

SCRUB

O la! O la! a footman have the spleen!

MRS. SULLEN

I thought that distemper had been only proper to people of
quality.   130

ARCHER

Madam, like all other fashions it wears out, and so descends
to their servants; though in a great many of us, I believe, it
proceeds from some melancholy particles in the blood,
occasioned by the stagnation of wages.

DORINDA

How affectedly the fellow talks!—How long, pray, have you   135
served your present master?

ARCHER

Not long; my life has been mostly spent in the service of the
ladies.

MRS. SULLEN

And pray, which service do you like best?

ARCHER

Madam, the ladies pay best; the honour of serving them is   140
sufficient wages; there is a charm in their looks that delivers
a pleasure with their commands, and gives our duty the wings
of inclination.

MRS. SULLEN

That flight was above the pitch of a livery.—And, sir,
would not you be satisfied to serve a lady again?   145

ARCHER

As a groom of the chamber, madam, but not as a footman.

MRS. SULLEN

I suppose you served as footman before?

ARCHER

For that reason I would not serve in that post again; for my
memory is too weak for the load of messages that the ladies
lay upon their servants in London. My Lady Howd'ye, the   150
last mistress I served, called me up one morning, and told
me, 'Martin, go to my Lady Allnight with my humble
service; tell her I was to wait on her ladyship yesterday, and
left word with Mrs. Rebecca, that the preliminaries of the

127 *spleen* dejection of spirits, melancholia

affair she knows of are stopped till we know the concurrence   155
of the person that I know of, for which there are circumstances wanting which we shall accommodate at the
old place; but that in the meantime there is a person about
her ladyship, that, from several hints and surmises, was
accessary at a certain time to the disappointments that   160
naturally attend things that to her knowledge are of more
importance—'

MRS. SULLEN }
DORINDA   } Ha! ha! ha! where are you going, sir?

ARCHER
Why, I han't half done!—The whole howd'ye was about
half an hour long; so I happened to misplace two syllables,   165
and was turned off and rendered incapable.

DORINDA
The pleasantest fellow, sister, I ever saw!—But, friend, if
your master be married, I presume you still serve a lady?

ARCHER
No, madam, I take care never to come into a married family;
the commands of the master and mistress are always so   170
contrary, that 'tis impossible to please both.

DORINDA (*Aside*)
There's a main point gained: my lord is not married, I find.

MRS. SULLEN
But I wonder, friend, that in so many good services you had
not a better provision made for you.

ARCHER
I don't know how, madam. I had a lieutenancy offered me   175
three or four times; but that is not bread, madam—I live
much better as I do.

SCRUB
Madam, he sings rarely! I was thought to do pretty well here
in the country till he came; but alack a day, I'm nothing to
my brother Martin!   180

DORINDA
Does he? Pray, sir, will you oblige us with a song?

ARCHER
Are you for passion or humour?

166 *rendered* represented or described as

---

175 *lieutenancy* Farquhar himself had been a lieutenant, much, it would
appear, to his own financial disadvantage—see Robert John Jordan,
'George Farquhar's Military Career', *Huntington Library Quarterly*, vol.
37 (1973–74), 251–64.

SCRUB

O le! he has the purest ballad about a trifle—

MRS. SULLEN

A trifle! pray, sir, let's have it.

ARCHER

I'm ashamed to offer you a trifle, madam; but since you   185
command me—

Sings to the tune of Sir Simon the King

A trifling song you shall hear,
Begun with a trifle and ended:
All trifling people draw near,
And I shall be nobly attended.   190

Were it not for trifles, a few,
That lately have come into play,
The men would want something to do,
And the women want something to say.

What makes men trifle in dressing?   195
Because the ladies (they know)
Admire, by often possessing,
That eminent trifle, a beau.

When the lover his moments has trifled,
The trifle of trifles to gain,   200
No sooner the virgin is rifled,
But a trifle shall part 'em again.

What mortal man would be able
At White's half an hour to sit?
Or who could bear a tea-table   205
Without talking of trifles for wit?

The court is from trifles secure;
Gold keys are no trifles, we see:
White rods are no trifles, I'm sure,
Whatever their bearers may be.   210

186 s.d. *Sir Simon the King* the title of a popular tune, first printed in
Playford's *Musick's Recreation* (1652); in *Tom Jones* (1749), Henry
Fielding made it one of Squire Western's favourites (Book 4, chapter 5).

208 *Gold keys* the insignia of the Lord Chamberlain, whose responsibilities
included the control of the playhouses.

209 *White rods* Both the Lord Chamberlain and the Lord High Treasurer
carried white staffs.

But if you will go to the place
Where trifles abundantly breed,
The levee will show you his Grace
Makes promises trifles indeed.

A coach with six footmen behind   215
I count neither trifle nor sin:
But, ye gods! how oft do we find
A scandalous trifle within.

A flask of champagne, people think it
A trifle, or something as bad: 220
But if you'll contrive how to drink it,
You'll find it no trifle, egad!

A parson's a trifle at sea,
A widow's a trifle in sorrow:
A peace is a trifle today;   225
Who knows what may happen tomorrow?

A black coat a trifle may cloak,
Or to hide it, the red may endeavour:
But if once the army is broke,
We shall have more trifles than ever.   230

The stage is a trifle, they say;
The reason pray carry along:

213 *levee* a morning assembly held by a prince or person of
distinction
227 *A black coat* worn by the clergy

---

213 *his Grace* It has been suggested, though without any real substantiation,
that Farquhar is here alluding to the duke of Ormonde's failure to
make good his promise to provide the needy dramatist with a captaincy.
225 *A peace* a mocking allusion to the Tory desire for an end to the
continental war.
229 *if once the army is broke* There was strong opposition in England in this
period to the maintenance of a substantial army in time of peace. After
the Treaty of Ryswick in 1697 (which had ended the last English
involvement in a continental war), Parliament had drastically reduced
the size of the standing army, and it was a reasonable prediction, in
1707, that similar action would be taken upon the conclusion of the
current war. For information on the continuing debate, see Lois G.
Schwoerer, 'The Literature of the Standing Army Controversy,
1697-1699', *Huntington Library Quarterly*, vol. 28 (1964-65), 187–212.

> Because at every new play
> The house they with trifles so throng.
>
> But with people's malice to trifle,   235
> And to set us all on a foot:
> The author of this is a trifle,
> And his song is a trifle to boot.

MRS. SULLEN

Very well, sir, we're obliged to you.—Something for a pair of
gloves.   *Offering him money*   240

ARCHER

I humbly beg leave to be excused: my master, madam, pays
me; nor dare I take money from any other hand, without
injuring his honour and disobeying his commands.

Exit

DORINDA

This is surprising! Did you ever see so pretty a well-bred
fellow?   245

MRS. SULLEN

The devil take him for wearing that livery!

DORINDA

I fancy, sister, he may be some gentleman, a friend of my
lord's, that his lordship has pitched upon for his courage,
fidelity, and discretion, to bear him company in this dress,
and who, ten to one, was his second too.   250

MRS. SULLEN

It is so, it must be so, and it shall be so!—for I like him.

DORINDA

What! better than the count?

MRS. SULLEN

The count happened to be the most agreeable man upon the
place; and so I chose him to serve me in my design upon my
husband. But I should like this fellow better in a design   255
upon myself.

DORINDA

But now, sister, for an interview with this lord and this
gentleman; how shall we bring that about?

MRS. SULLEN

Patience! you country ladies give no quarter, if once you be
entered. Would you prevent their desires, and give the   260
fellows no wishing-time? Look ye, Dorinda, if my Lord

260 *entered* engaged in action
260 *prevent* anticipate

Aimwell loves you or deserves you, he'll find a way to see
you, and there we must leave it. My business comes now
upon the tapis. Have you prepared your brother?

DORINDA

Yes, yes.   265

MRS. SULLEN

And how did he relish it?

DORINDA

He said little, mumbled something to himself, promised to
be guided by me—but here he comes.

Enter SULLEN

SULLEN

What singing was that I heard just now?

MRS. SULLEN

The singing in your head, my dear; you complained of it all   270
day.

SULLEN

You're impertinent.

MRS. SULLEN

I was ever so, since I became one flesh with you.

SULLEN

One flesh! rather two carcasses joined unnaturally together.

MRS. SULLEN

Or rather a living soul coupled to a dead body.   275

DORINDA

So, this is fine encouragement for me!

SULLEN

Yes, my wife shows you what you must do.

MRS. SULLEN

And my husband shows you what you must suffer.

SULLEN

'Sdeath, why can't you be silent?

264 *upon the tapis* literally, upon the table-cloth; under discussion or
   consideration

274–5 *One flesh . . .* Cf. Milton's 'nay, instead of being one flesh, they will be
   rather two carcasses chained unnaturally together; or, as it may happen, a living soul bound to a dead corpse' (*Prose Works*, III, 249).

275 *living soul coupled to a dead body* Clearly she thinks of herself as the
   living soul and is thus cheerfully inverting the language traditional in
   the period's discussions of marriage, in which the husband is conventionally seen as the soul and the wife as the body—see Rosalie E.
   Osmond, 'Body, Soul, and the Marriage Relationship', *Journal of the
   History of Ideas*, vol. 34 (1973), 283–90.

MRS. SULLEN

'Sdeath, why can't you talk?   280

SULLEN

Do you talk to any purpose?

MRS. SULLEN

Do you think to any purpose?

SULLEN

Sister, hark ye—(*Whispers*)—I shan't be home till it be
late.   *Exit*

MRS. SULLEN

What did he whisper to ye?   285

DORINDA

That he would go round the back way, come into the closet,
and listen as I directed him. But let me beg you once more,
dear sister, to drop this project; for, as I told you before,
instead of awaking him to kindness, you may provoke him to
a rage; and then who knows how far his brutality may carry   290
him?

MRS. SULLEN

I'm provided to receive him, I warrant you. But here comes
the count: vanish!   *Exit* DORINDA

Enter COUNT BELLAIR

Don't you wonder, Monsieur le Count, that I was not at
church this afternoon?   295

COUNT BELLAIR

I more wonder, madam, that you go dere at all, or how you
dare to lift those eyes to Heaven that are guilty of so much
killing.

MRS. SULLEN

If Heaven, sir, has given to my eyes with the power of
killing the virtue of making a cure, I hope the one may   300
atone for the other.

COUNT BELLAIR

O largely, madam, would your ladyship be as ready to
apply the remedy as to give the wound. Consider, madam,
I am doubly a prisoner; first to the arms of your general,
then to your more conquering eyes. My first chains are easy   305
—there a ransom may redeem me; but from your fetters I
never shall get free.

MRS. SULLEN

Alas, sir! why should you complain to me of your captivity,
who am in chains myself? You know, sir, that I am bound,
nay, must be tied up in that particular that might give you   310

ease: I am like you, a prisoner of war—of war, indeed,—I
have given my parole of honour! Would you break yours to
gain your liberty?

COUNT BELLAIR

Most certainly I would, were I a prisoner among the Turks:
dis is your case; you're a slave, madam, slave to the worst of　315
Turks, a husband.

MRS. SULLEN

There lies my foible, I confess; no fortifications, no courage,
conduct, nor vigilancy can pretend to defend a place, where
the cruelty of the governor forces the garrison to mutiny.

COUNT BELLAIR

And where de besieger is resolved to die before de place.　320
Here will I fix;—(*Kneels*) with tears, vows, and prayers
assault your heart, and never rise till you surrender; or if I
must storm—Love and St. Michael!—And so I begin the
attack.

MRS. SULLEN

Stand off!—(*Aside*) Sure he hears me not!—And I could　325
almost wish he—did not!—The fellow makes love very
prettily. [*To* COUNT BELLAIR] But, sir, why should you put
such a value upon my person, when you see it despised by
one that knows it so much better?

COUNT BELLAIR

He knows it not, though he possesses it; if he but knew the　330
value of the jewel he is master of, he would always wear it
next his heart, and sleep with it in his arms.

MRS. SULLEN

But since he throws me unregarded from him—

COUNT BELLAIR

And one that knows your value well comes by and takes you
up, is it not justice?　　　　　　　　*Goes to lay hold on her*　335

312 *parole of honour* word of honour; the undertaking given by a prisoner-
of-war that he will not try to escape, or that, if liberated, he will return
to custody under stated conditions, or will refrain from taking up arms
against his captors for a stated period (OED).

314 *the Turks* The conviction persisted that 'the Turk was a species
different in *kind* from Christian states whether Catholic or Protestant, a
political pariah excluded by his very nature from membership in the
family of European states' (F. L. Baumer, 'England, the Turk, and the
Common Corps of Christendom', *English Historical Review*, vol. 50
(1944–45), 27). Accordingly, it was possible to argue, as the Count does
here, that, in dealing with the Turks, the normal standards regulating a
Christian's dealings with his fellow believers could be suspended.

Enter SULLEN *with his sword drawn*

SULLEN

Hold, villain, hold!

MRS. SULLEN (*Presenting a pistol*)

Do you hold!

SULLEN

What! murder your husband to defend your bully!

MRS. SULLEN

Bully! for shame, Mr. Sullen. Bullies wear long swords; the
gentleman has none; he's a prisoner, you know. I was aware   340
of your outrage, and prepared this to receive your violence,
and, if occasion were, to preserve myself against the force of
this other gentleman.

COUNT BELLAIR

O madam, your eyes be bettre firearms than your pistol;
they nevre miss.   345

SULLEN

What! court my wife to my face!

MRS. SULLEN

Pray, Mr. Sullen, put up; suspend your fury for a minute.

SULLEN

To give you time to invent an excuse!

MRS. SULLEN

I need none.

SULLEN

No, for I heard every syllable of your discourse.   350

COUNT BELLAIR

Ay! and begar, I tink de dialogue was vera pretty.

MRS. SULLEN

Then I suppose, sir, you heard something of your own
barbarity.

SULLEN

Barbarity! 'Oons, what does the woman call barbarity? Do I
ever meddle with you?   355

MRS. SULLEN

No.

SULLEN

As for you, sir, I shall take another time.

COUNT BELLAIR

Ah, begar, and so must I.

338 *bully* the 'gallant' or protector of a prostitute
351 *begar* 'By God'

SULLEN

Look'ee, madam, don't think that my anger proceeds from
any concern I have for your honour, but for my own; and if 360
you can contrive any way of being a whore without making
me a cuckold, do it and welcome.

MRS. SULLEN

Sir, I thank you kindly; you would allow me the sin but rob
me of the pleasure. No, no, I'm resolved never to venture
upon the crime without the satisfaction of seeing you 365
punished for't.

SULLEN

Then will you grant me this, my dear? Let anybody else do
you the favour but that Frenchman, for I mortally hate his
whole generation.   *Exit*

COUNT BELLAIR

Ah, sir, that be ungrateful, for, begar, I love some of yours.— 370
Madam—   *Approaching her*

MRS. SULLEN

No, sir.

COUNT BELLAIR

No, sir! Garzoon, madam, I am not your husband.

MRS. SULLEN

'Tis time to undeceive you, sir. I believed your addresses to
me were no more than an amusement, and I hope you will 375
think the same of my complaisance; and to convince you that
you ought, you must know that I brought you hither only
to make you instrumental in setting me right with my
husband, for he was planted to listen by my appointment.

COUNT BELLAIR

By your appointment?   380

MRS. SULLEN

Certainly.

COUNT BELLAIR

And so, madam, while I was telling twenty stories to part you
from your husband, begar, I was bringing you together all
the while?

MRS. SULLEN

I ask your pardon, sir, but I hope this will give you a taste of 385
the virtue of the English ladies.

COUNT BELLAIR

Begar, madam, your virtue be vera great, but garzoon, your
honeste be vera little.

373 *Garzoon* 'God's wounds'

Enter DORINDA

MRS. SULLEN

Nay, now you're angry, sir.

COUNT BELLAIR

Angry!—*Fair Dorinda* (*Sings* DORINDA *the opera tune, and*   390
addresses to DORINDA). Madam, when your ladyship want a
fool, send for me. *Fair Dorinda, Revenge, etc.*   *Exit*

MRS. SULLEN

There goes the true humour of his nation—resentment with
good manners, and the height of anger in a song!—Well,
sister, you must be judge, for you have heard the trial.   395

DORINDA

And I bring in my brother guilty.

MRS. SULLEN

But I must bear the punishment. 'Tis hard, sister.

DORINDA

I own it; but you must have patience.

MRS. SULLEN

Patience! the cant of custom—Providence sends no evil without a remedy. Should I lie groaning under a yoke I can shake   400
off, I were accessary to my ruin, and my patience were no
better than self-murder.

390 *Fair Dorinda* The song referred to has never been satisfactorily identified. Perhaps the best suggestion yet made is that Farquhar has in
mind a song added in performance to the Dryden/Davenant *Tempest*
(first performed in 1667), these Restoration revisers of Shakespeare's
work having provided Miranda with a sister called Dorinda.

393 *humour of his nation* There was a great deal of eighteenth-century
commentary on the alleged capacity of the French to remain gay and
apparently unruffled in the most adverse of circumstances. In
Addison's account, France was a country where 'Everyone Sings
Laughs and Starves'—see, for this and similar quotations, John G.
Hayman, 'Notions on National Characters in the Eighteenth Century',
Huntington Library Quarterly, vol. 35 (1971–72), 5–6.

399 *Patience! the cant of custom* Cf. the comments of Thomas Forde on
Milton's arguments for divorce: 'it is not in the power of a man to
dis-joyn himself from the companion which providence hath *joyned* him
to, in so indissoluble a link of amitie, that one member is not more
truly a part of a mans body than his *Wife*; and therefore he ought rather
to *undergoe* with patience what God hath ordained him, perhaps for
other reasons than he can understand, than to *forgoe* it with wilfulnesse'
(J. Milton French (ed.), *The Life Records of John Milton*, vol. 4 (New
Brunswick, New Jersey, 1956), 342).

DORINDA

But how can you shake off the yoke? Your divisions don't
come within the reach of the law for a divorce.

MRS. SULLEN

Law! What law can search into the remote abyss of nature?   405
What evidence can prove the unaccountable disaffections of
wedlock? Can a jury sum up the endless aversions that are
rooted in our souls, or can a bench give judgment upon
antipathies?

DORINDA

They never pretended, sister; they never meddle but in case   410
of uncleanness.

MRS. SULLEN

Uncleanness! O sister! casual violation is a transient injury,
and may possibly be repaired, but can radical hatreds be
ever reconciled? No, no, sister, nature is the first lawgiver,
and when she has set tempers opposite, not all the golden   415
links of wedlock nor iron manacles of law can keep 'em fast.

Wedlock we own ordained by Heaven's decree,
But such as Heaven ordained it first to be—
Concurring tempers in the man and wife
As mutual helps to draw the load of life.   420
View all the works of Providence above:
The stars with harmony and concord move.
View all the works of Providence below:
The fire, the water, earth, and air, we know,
All in one plant agree to make it grow.   425

406–7 *disaffections of wedlock* Cf. Milton's view that God did not authorize
    'a judicial court to toss about and divulge the unaccountable and secret
    reason of dissaffection between man and wife, as a thing most improperly
    answerable to any such kind of trial' (*Prose Works*, III, 263).
412–14 *casual violation . . . the first lawgiver* Cf. Milton: 'natural hatred
    whenever it arises, is a greater evil in marriage than the accident of
    adultery, a greater defrauding, a greater injustice' (*Prose Works*, III,
    254); 'they [men] would be juster in their balancing between natural
    hatred and casual adultery; this being but a transient injury, and soon
    amended . . . but that other being an unspeakable and unremitting
    sorrow and offence' (ibid., 254); 'to forbid dislike against the guiltless
    instinct of nature, is not within the province of any law to reach' (ibid.,
    265).
415–16 *golden links . . . iron manacles* Cf. Milton: 'To couple hatred there-
    fore, though wedlock try all her golden links, and borrow to her aid all
    the iron manacles and fetters of the law, it does but seek to twist a rope
    of sand' (*Prose Works*, III, 265).

Must man, the chiefest work of art divine,
Be doomed in endless discord to repine?
No, we should injure Heaven by that surmise:
Omnipotence is just, were man but wise.   [*Exeunt*]

Act IV, [Scene i]

Scene continues
Enter MRS. SULLEN

MRS. SULLEN

Were I born an humble Turk, where women have no soul
nor property, there I must sit contented. But in England,
a country whose women are its glory, must women be abused?
where women rule, must women be enslaved? Nay, cheated
into slavery, mocked by a promise of comfortable society into   5
a wilderness of solitude! I dare not keep the thought about
me. O, here comes something to divert me.

Enter a COUNTRY WOMAN

COUNTRY WOMAN

I come, an't please your ladyship—you're my Lady
Bountiful, an't ye?

MRS. SULLEN

Well, good woman, go on.   10

COUNTRY WOMAN

I come seventeen long mail to have a cure for my husband's
sore leg.

MRS. SULLEN

Your husband! What, woman, cure your husband!

COUNTRY WOMAN

Ay, poor man, for his sore leg won't let him stir from home.

MRS. SULLEN

There, I confess, you have given me a reason. Well, good   15
woman, I'll tell you what you must do. You must lay your

429 [*Exeunt*] Q follows the last dialogue of the scene with '*End of the
     Third Act*'
  5 *comfortable* providing mental and spiritual support and strength
  8 *ladyship* ed. (Ladyships Q)

---

  1 *an humble Turk* For a characteristically Restoration version of the
     Turkish way with women, see Rochester's *A Very Heroical Epistle in
     Answer to Ephelia*, lines 32ff.
  4 *where women rule* In 1707, as Farquhar duly celebrates in the prologue,
     Queen Anne was on the throne, and the Glorious Revolution of 1688
     had ushered in the joint rule of William and Mary.

husband's leg upon a table, and with a chopping knife you
must lay it open as broad as you can; then you must take
out the bone, and beat the flesh soundly with a rolling pin;
then take salt, pepper, cloves, mace, and ginger, some sweet   20
herbs, and season it very well; then roll it up like brawn, and
put it into the oven for two hours.

COUNTRY WOMAN

Heavens reward your ladyship!—I have two little babies too
that are piteous bad with the graips, an't please ye.

MRS. SULLEN

Put a little pepper and salt in their bellies, good woman.   25

Enter LADY BOUNTIFUL

I beg your ladyship's pardon for taking your business out of
your hands; I have been a-tampering here a little with one
of your patients.

LADY BOUNTIFUL

Come, good woman, don't mind this mad creature; I am the
person that you want, I suppose. What would you have,   30
woman?

MRS. SULLEN

She wants something for her husband's sore leg.

LADY BOUNTIFUL

What's the matter with his leg, goody?

COUNTRY WOMAN

It come first, as one might say, with a sort of dizziness in his
foot, then he had a kind of a laziness in his joints, and then   35
his leg broke out, and then it swelled, and then it closed
again, and then it broke out again, and then it festered, and
then it grew better, and then it grew worse again.

MRS. SULLEN

Ha! ha! ha!

LADY BOUNTIFUL

How can you be merry with the misfortunes of other   40
people?

MRS. SULLEN

Because my own make me sad, madam.

LADY BOUNTIFUL

The worst reason in the world, daughter; your own misfortunes should teach you to pity others.

---

24 *graips* colic pains, gripes
33 *goody* a civil mode of address applied to a woman of humble rank

MRS. SULLEN

But the woman's misfortunes and mine are nothing alike; 45
her husband is sick, and mine, alas, is in health.

LADY BOUNTIFUL

What! would you wish your husband sick?

MRS. SULLEN

Not of a sore leg, of all things.

LADY BOUNTIFUL

Well, good woman, go to the pantry, get your bellyful of
victuals; then I'll give you a receipt of diet-drink for your 50
husband. But d'ye hear, goody, you must not let your husband
move too much.

COUNTRY WOMAN

No, no, madam, the poor man's inclinable enough to lie still.

Exit

LADY BOUNTIFUL

Well, daughter Sullen, though you laugh, I have done
miracles about the country here with my receipts. 55

MRS. SULLEN

Miracles indeed, if they have cured anybody; but I believe,
madam, the patient's faith goes farther toward the miracle
than your prescription.

LADY BOUNTIFUL

Fancy helps in some cases; but there's your husband,
who has as little fancy as anybody, I brought him from 60
death's door.

MRS. SULLEN

I suppose, madam, you made him drink plentifully of ass's
milk.

Enter DORINDA [*who*] *runs to* MRS. SULLEN

DORINDA

News, dear sister! news! news!

Enter ARCHER, *running*

ARCHER

Where, where is my Lady Bountiful?—Pray, which is the old 65
lady of you three?

---

50 *receipt* recipe

62–3 *ass's milk* often prescribed by eighteenth-century doctors as a di-
gestive; Mrs Sullen's retort might be construed innocently by her naive
mother-in-law (Rothstein).

LADY BOUNTIFUL

I am.

ARCHER

O madam, the fame of your ladyship's charity, goodness,
benevolence, skill, and ability, have drawn me hither to
implore your ladyship's help in behalf of my unfortunate 70
master, who is this moment breathing his last.

LADY BOUNTIFUL

Your master! where is he?

ARCHER

At your gate, madam. Drawn by the appearance of your
handsome house to view it nearer, and walking up the
avenue within five paces of the courtyard, he was taken ill of 75
a sudden with a sort of I know not what; but down he fell,
and there he lies.

LADY BOUNTIFUL

Here, Scrub! Gipsy! all run, get my easy chair down stairs,
put the gentleman in it, and bring him in quickly, quickly!

ARCHER

Heaven will reward your ladyship for this charitable act. 80

LADY BOUNTIFUL

Is your master used to these fits?

ARCHER

O yes, madam, frequently: I have known him have five or
six of a night.

LADY BOUNTIFUL

What's his name?

ARCHER

Lord, madam, he's a-dying! A minute's care or neglect may 85
save or destroy his life.

LADY BOUNTIFUL

Ah, poor gentleman!—Come, friend, show me the way; I'll
see him brought in myself.   *Exit with* ARCHER

DORINDA

O sister, my heart flutters about strangely! I can hardly
forbear running to his assistance. 90

MRS. SULLEN

And I'll lay my life he deserves your assistance more than he
wants it. Did not I tell you that my lord would find a way to
come at you? Love's his distemper, and you must be the
physician; put on all your charms, summon all your fire into
your eyes, plant the whole artillery of your looks against his 95
breast, and down with him.

DORINDA

O sister! I'm but a young gunner; I shall be afraid to shoot,
for fear the piece should recoil and hurt myself.

MRS. SULLEN

Never fear: you shall see me shoot before you, if you will.

DORINDA

No, no, dear sister; you have missed your mark so unfortun-   100
ately, that I shan't care for being instructed by you.

Enter AIMWELL *in a chair, carried by* ARCHER *and* SCRUB, LADY
BOUNTIFUL, GIPSY—AIMWELL *counterfeiting a swoon*

LADY BOUNTIFUL

Here, here, let's see the hartshorn drops.—Gipsy, a glass of
fair water! His fit's very strong.—Bless me, how his hands
are clinched!

ARCHER

For shame, ladies, what d'ye do? Why don't you help us?—   105
(*To* DORINDA) Pray, madam, take his hand, and open it, if you
can, whilst I hold his head.

DORINDA *takes his hand*

DORINDA

Poor gentleman!—O!—he has got my hand within his, and
squeezes it unmercifully—

LADY BOUNTIFUL

'Tis the violence of his convulsion, child.   110

ARCHER

O madam, he's perfectly possessed in these cases—he'll bite
if you don't have a care.

DORINDA

O, my hand! my hand!

LADY BOUNTIFUL

What's the matter with the foolish girl? I have got this hand
open, you see, with a great deal of ease.   115

ARCHER

Ay, but, madam, your daughter's hand is somewhat warmer

---

98 *piece* gun
102 *hartshorn drops* smelling salts obtained from the horn of the hart
103 *fair water* pure water

than your ladyship's, and the heat of it draws the force of the
spirits that way.

MRS. SULLEN

I find, friend, you're very learned in these sorts of fits.

ARCHER

'Tis no wonder, madam, for I'm often troubled with them   120
myself; I find myself extremely ill at this minute.

Looking hard at MRS. SULLEN

MRS. SULLEN (*Aside*)

I fancy I could find a way to cure you.

LADY BOUNTIFUL

His fit holds him very long.

ARCHER

Longer than usual, madam.—Pray, young lady, open his
breast, and give him air.   125

LADY BOUNTIFUL

Where did his illness take him first, pray?

ARCHER

Today at church, madam.

LADY BOUNTIFUL

In what manner was he taken?

ARCHER

Very strangely, my lady. He was of a sudden touched with
something in his eyes, which, at the first, he only felt, but   130
could not tell whether 'twas pain or pleasure.

LADY BOUNTIFUL

Wind, nothing but wind!

ARCHER

By soft degrees it grew and mounted to his brain, there his
fancy caught it; there formed it so beautiful, and dressed it
up in such gay pleasing colours, that his transported appetite   135
seized the fair idea, and straight conveyed it to his heart.
That hospitable seat of life sent all its sanguine spirits forth
to meet, and opened all its sluicy gates to take the stranger in.

LADY BOUNTIFUL

Your master should never go without a bottle to smell to.—
O, he recovers!—The lavender water—some feathers to burn   140

117–18 *the spirits* Two varieties of spirit were believed to circulate in the
human body. The kind Farquhar probably had in mind was called vital
spirit and was regarded as 'the vehicle of the natural heat and moisture
which are essential to life'. See Lawrence Babb, *The Elizabethan
Malady: A Study of Melancholia in English Literature from 1580 to 1642*
(East Lansing, 1951), p.8.

under his nose—Hungary-water to rub his temples.—O, he
comes to himself!—Hem a little, sir, hem.—Gipsy, bring the
cordial-water.   AIMWELL *seems to awake in amaze*

DORINDA

How d'ye, sir?

AIMWELL

Where am I?   *Rising*   145
Sure I have passed the gulf of silent death,
And now I land on the Elysian shore!—
Behold the goddess of those happy plains,
Fair Proserpine—let me adore thy bright divinity.
                Kneels to DORINDA *and kisses her hand*

MRS. SULLEN

So, so, so! I knew where the fit would end!   150

AIMWELL

Eurydice perhaps—
How could thy Orpheus keep his word,
And not look back upon thee?
No treasure but thyself could sure have bribed him
To look one minute off thee.   155

LADY BOUNTIFUL

Delirious, poor gentleman!

ARCHER

Very delirious, madam, very delirious.

AIMWELL

Martin's voice, I think.

ARCHER

Yes, my lord.—How does your lordship?

LADY BOUNTIFUL

Lord! did you mind that, girls?   160

AIMWELL

Where am I?

ARCHER

In very good hands, sir. You were taken just now with one of
your old fits under the trees just by this good lady's house;
her ladyship had you taken in, and has miraculously brought
you to yourself, as you see.   165

AIMWELL

I am so confounded with shame, madam, that I can now only

---

141 *Hungary-water* tincture of rosemary flowers

---

149 *Proserpine* daughter of Ceres, to whom Aimwell has already rhapso-
dically compared Dorinda, and goddess of Elysium, the joyful under-
world.

beg pardon—and refer my acknowledgments for your
ladyship's care till an opportunity offers of making some
amends. I dare be no longer troublesome.—Martin, give two
guineas to the servants.   *Going*   170

DORINDA

Sir, you may catch cold by going so soon into the air; you
don't look, sir, as if you were perfectly recovered.

Here ARCHER *talks to* LADY BOUNTIFUL *in dumb show*

AIMWELL

That I shall never be, madam; my present illness is so rooted,
that I must expect to carry it to my grave.

MRS. SULLEN

Don't despair, sir; I have known several in your distemper   175
shake it off with a fortnight's physic.

LADY BOUNTIFUL

Come, sir, your servant has been telling me that you're apt to
relapse if you go into the air. Your good manners shan't get
the better of ours—you shall sit down again, sir. Come, sir,
we don't mind ceremonies in the country—here, sir, my   180
service t'ye.—You shall taste my water; 'tis a cordial, I can
assure you, and of my own making—drink it off, sir.
(AIMWELL *drinks*) And how d'ye find yourself now, sir?

AIMWELL

Somewhat better—though very faint still.

LADY BOUNTIFUL

Ay, ay, people are always faint after these fits.—Come, girls, 185
you shall show the gentleman the house.—'Tis but an old
family building, sir; but you had better walk about and cool
by degrees than venture immediately into the air. You'll
find some tolerable pictures.—Dorinda, show the gentleman
the way. I must go to the poor woman below.   *Exit*   190

DORINDA

This way, sir.

AIMWELL

Ladies, shall I beg leave for my servant to wait on you, for he
understands pictures very well?

MRS. SULLEN

Sir, we understand originals as well as he does pictures,
so he may come along.   195

---

194 *originals* Mrs Sullen is punning on two meanings of the word:
(1) people of singular or eccentric disposition (2) original works
of art

Exeunt DORINDA, MRS. SULLEN, AIMWELL, ARCHER [, GIPSY]
        —AIMWELL *leads* DORINDA

Enter FOIGARD *and* SCRUB, *meeting*

FOIGARD

Save you, Master Scrub!

SCRUB

Sir, I won't be saved your way—I hate a priest, I abhor the
French, and I defy the devil. Sir, I'm a bold Briton, and will
spill the last drop of my blood to keep out popery and
slavery.   200

FOIGARD

Master Scrub, you would put me down in politics, and so I
would be speaking with Mrs. Shipsey.

SCRUB

Good Mr. Priest, you can't speak with her; she's sick, sir;
she's gone abroad, sir; she's—dead two months ago, sir.

Enter GIPSY

GIPSY

How now, impudence! How dare you talk so saucily to the   205
doctor? Pray, sir, don't take it ill; for the common people
of England are not so civil to strangers, as—

SCRUB

You lie! you lie! 'tis the common people that are civilest to
strangers.

GIPSY

Sirrah, I have a good mind to—Get you out, I say!   210

SCRUB

I won't.

GIPSY

You won't, saucebox!—Pray, doctor, what is the captain's
name that came to your inn last night?

SCRUB

The captain! Ah, the devil, there she hampers me again; the
captain has me on one side, and the priest on t'other: so   215

---

198 *bold Briton* A topic frequently celebrated in contemporary political
    pamphlets is the felicity of Englishmen in 'being Freemen and not
    Slaves in this unhappy Age, when an universal Deluge of Tyranny has
    overspread the face of the whole Earth' (*An Argument, Shewing, that a
    Standing Army Is inconsistent with A Free Government* (London, 1697),
    p.2). The most formidable external threat to this freedom was considered
    by many writers to be the aggressive Catholicism of the France of
    Louis XIV.

between the gown and the sword, I have a fine time on't.—
But, *Cedunt arma togae.*   *Going*

GIPSY

What, sirrah, won't you march?

SCRUB

No, my dear, I won't march—but I'll walk.—[*Aside*] And
I'll make bold to listen a little too.   220
                    Goes behind the side-scene and listens

GIPSY

Indeed, doctor, the count has been barbarously treated, that's
the truth on't.

FOIGARD

Ah, Mrs. Gipsy, upon my shoul, now, gra, his complainings
would mollify the marrow in your bones, and move the
bowels of your commiseration! He veeps, and he dances,   225
and he fistles, and he swears, and he laughs, and he
stamps, and he sings; in conclusion, joy, he's afflicted *à la
François*, and a stranger would not know whider to cry or
to laugh with him.

GIPSY

What would you have me do, doctor?   230

FOIGARD

Noting, joy, but only hide the count in Mrs. Sullen's closet
when it is dark.

GIPSY

Nothing! Is that nothing? It would be both a sin and a
shame, doctor.

FOIGARD

Here is twenty louis d'ors, joy, for your shame, and I will   235

235 *louis d'ors* a gold coin issued in the reign of Louis XIII and sub-
     sequently till the time of Louis XVI
_____

217 *Cedunt arma togae* the sword gives way to the gown—the phrase (with a
     slight adjustment of tense) derives from Cicero, *De Officiis*, I, 22.
     Strauss considered it indecorous that Scrub should be allowed to rise
     to Latin, but this affectation is surely of a piece with his pretensions
     to gentility.
220 s.d. *side-scene* the name for free-standing, tall, narrow pieces of scenery,
     which, projecting from the wings, framed the back-scene on either side
     of the stage; for further information about them, see Richard Southern,
     Changeable Scenery: Its Origin and Development in the British Theatre
     (London, 1952).
223 *gra* a ghráidh, Irish for love, dear—often given in playtexts of the
     period to Irish characters.

give you an absolution for the shin.

GIPSY

But won't that money look like a bribe?

FOIGARD

Dat is according as you shall tauk it. If you receive the
money beforehand, 'twill be *logicé* a bribe; but, if you stay
till afterwards, 'twill be only a gratification.   240

GIPSY

Well, doctor, I'll take it *logicé*.—But what must I do with
my conscience, sir?

FOIGARD

Leave dat wid me, joy; I am your priest, gra; and your
conscience is under my hands.

GIPSY

But should I put the count into the closet—   245

FOIGARD

Vel, is dere any shin for a man's being in a closhet? One
may go to prayers in a closhet.

GIPSY

But if the lady should come into her chamber, and go to bed?

FOIGARD

Vel, and is dere any shin in going to bed, joy?

GIPSY

Ay, but if the parties should meet, doctor?   250

FOIGARD

Vel den—the parties must be responsible. Do you be after
putting the count in the closet; and leave the shins wid
themselves. I will come with the count to instruct you in
your chamber.

GIPSY

Well, doctor, your religion is so pure! Methinks I'm so easy   255
after an absolution, and can sin afresh with so much security,
that I'm resolved to die a martyr to't. Here's the key of the

---

239 *logicé* according to logic
240 *gratification* gratuity

---

236 *absolution* It was an often-repeated Protestant allegation that Roman
priests were prepared to offer absolution for sins with facile alacrity
and that they were also masters of a conscience-soothing rhetoric which
could provide spiritual justifications even for murder. Catholic apologists continually strove to combat the effect of such slanders—see, for
example, *Somers Tracts*, vol. I (London, 1748), 45.

garden door: come in the back way when 'tis late; I'll be
ready to receive you. But don't so much as whisper; only
take hold of my hand; I'll lead you, and do you lead the   260
count, and follow me.   *Exeunt*

Enter SCRUB

SCRUB
What witchcraft now have these two imps of the devil been
a-hatching here? There's twenty louis d'ors; I heard that,
and saw the purse.—But I must give room to my betters.
                                                        [*Exit*]

Enter AIMWELL *leading* DORINDA, *and making love in dumb show;*
MRS. SULLEN *and* ARCHER

MRS. SULLEN (*To* ARCHER)
Pray, sir, how d'ye like that piece?   265
ARCHER
O, 'tis Leda! You find, madam, how Jupiter comes dis-
guised to make love—
MRS. SULLEN
But what think you there of Alexander's battles?
ARCHER
We want only a Le Brun, madam, to draw greater battles
and a greater general of our own. The Danube, madam,   270
would make a greater figure in a picture than the Granicus;
and we have our Ramillies to match their Arbela.
MRS. SULLEN
Pray, sir, what head is that in the corner there?
ARCHER
O madam, 'tis poor Ovid in his exile.

265 *Pray, sir, how d'ye like that piece?* For a comment on gallery scenes of a
    kindred type, see Jean H. Hagstrum, *The Sister Arts: the Tradition of
    Literary Pictorialism and English Poetry from Dryden to Gray* (Chicago
    and London, 1958), pp.238–9.
266 *Leda* Leda was raped by Jupiter in the guise of a swan.
269 *Le Brun* Charles Le Brun (1619–90), the French court painter, whose
    works included a famous series of paintings of the battles of Alexander.
    Archer contrasts the victories of Marlborough, 'a greater general of our
    own', at Blenheim (on the Danube) in 1704 and at Ramillies in 1706
    with those of Alexander at the Granicus and Arbela, both of which had
    been portrayed by Le Brun.
274 *poor Ovid* Ovid was banished from Rome to Tomis by Augustus; the
    obscurity of the reasons for this action has bred much speculation and
    many theories. Archer, of course, chooses one convenient to his present
    purposes.

MRS. SULLEN

What was he banished for?   275

ARCHER

His ambitious love, madam.—(*Bowing*) His misfortune touches me.

MRS. SULLEN

Was he successful in his amours?

ARCHER

There he has left us in the dark. He was too much a gentleman to tell.   280

MRS. SULLEN

If he were secret, I pity him.

ARCHER

And if he were successful, I envy him.

MRS. SULLEN

How d'ye like that Venus over the chimney?

ARCHER

Venus! I protest, madam, I took it for your picture; but now I look again, 'tis not handsome enough.   285

MRS. SULLEN

O, what a charm is flattery! If you would see my picture, there it is—over that cabinet. How d'ye like it?

ARCHER

I must admire anything, madam, that has the least resemblance of you. But, methinks, madam—(*He looks at the picture and* MRS. SULLEN *three or four times, by turns*) Pray,   290
madam, who drew it?

MRS. SULLEN

A famous hand, sir.   *Here* AIMWELL *and* DORINDA *go off*

ARCHER

A famous hand, madam!—Your eyes, indeed, are featured there; but where's the sparkling moisture, shining fluid, in which they swim? The picture, indeed, has your dimples;   295
but where's the swarm of killing Cupids that should ambush there? The lips too are figured out; but where's the carnation dew, the pouting ripeness, that tempts the taste in the original?

MRS. SULLEN [*Aside*]

Had it been my lot to have matched with such a man!   300

ARCHER

Your breasts too—presumptuous man! What, paint Heaven!

---

301 *Your breasts* A rather striking decolletage was characteristic of many late seventeenth-century portraits of fashionable ladies.

—Apropos, madam, in the very next picture is Salmoneus,
that was struck dead with lightning for offering to imitate
Jove's thunder; I hope you served the painter so, madam?

MRS. SULLEN

Had my eyes the power of thunder, they should employ   305
their lightning better.

ARCHER

There's the finest bed in that room, madam! I suppose 'tis
your ladyship's bedchamber.

MRS. SULLEN

And what then, sir?

ARCHER

I think the quilt is the richest that ever I saw. I can't at this   310
distance, madam, distinguish the figures of the embroidery.
Will you give me leave, madam?

MRS. SULLEN

[*Aside*] The devil take his impudence!—Sure, if I gave
him an opportunity, he durst not offer it?—I have a great
mind to try.—(*Going: returns*) 'Sdeath, what am I doing?—   315
And alone, too!—Sister! sister!   *Runs out*

ARCHER

I'll follow her close—
For where a Frenchman durst attempt to storm,
A Briton sure may well the work perform.   *Going*

Enter SCRUB

SCRUB

Martin! brother Martin!   320

ARCHER

O, brother Scrub, I beg your pardon; I was not a-going;
here's a guinea my master ordered you.

SCRUB

A guinea! hi! hi! hi! a guinea! eh—by this light it is a
guinea! But I suppose you expect one and twenty shillings
in change?   325

ARCHER

Not at all; I have another for Gipsy.

---

302 *Salmoneus* a son of Aeolus and brother of Sisyphus, who built the town
of Salome in Elis. His arrogance was such that he caused sacrifices to
be offered to himself and imitated the thunder of Zeus, who killed him
with a thunderbolt and destroyed his town (Jeffares).

SCRUB

A guinea for her! Faggot and fire for the witch!—Sir, give
me that guinea, and I'll discover a plot.

ARCHER

A plot!

SCRUB

Ay, sir, a plot, and a horrid plot! First, it must be a plot, be-   330
cause there's a woman in't; secondly, it must be a plot, because
there's a priest in't; thirdly, it must be a plot, because there's
French gold in't; and fourthly, it must be a plot, because
I don't know what to make on't.

ARCHER

Nor anybody else, I'm afraid, brother Scrub.   335

SCRUB

Truly, I'm afraid so too; for where there's a priest and a
woman, there's always a mystery and a riddle. This I know,
that here has been the doctor with a temptation in one hand
and an absolution in the other, and Gipsy has sold herself
to the devil; I saw the price paid down, my eyes shall take   340
their oath on't.

ARCHER

And is all this bustle about Gipsy?

SCRUB

That's not all; I could hear but a word here and there; but
I remember they mentioned a count, a closet, a back door,
and a key.   345

ARCHER

The count! Did you hear nothing of Mrs. Sullen?

SCRUB

I did hear some word that sounded that way; but whether
it was Sullen or Dorinda, I could not distinguish.

328 *a plot* Scrub's suspicions appear to be influenced by memories of the
Popish Plot of Charles II's reign, a crisis most fully described in John
Kenyon's *The Popish Plot* (London, 1972). On that occasion, the main
rumours and allegations, concerning a plot (fuelled by French gold) to
assassinate Charles II, were accompanied by many lesser scare-
stories—including, for example, one about a maidservant who con-
fessed to having set fire to her master's house 'at the instigation of a
popish priest' (Narcissus Luttrell, *A Brief Historical Relation Of State
Affairs From September 1678 To April 1714* (Oxford, 1857), vol. 1, 9).
Accusations concerning the influence of French *louis d'ors* upon English
politics were still common in the early years of the eighteenth
century—see, for example, G. M. Trevelyan, *England Under Queen
Anne: Blenheim* (London, 1948), p.136.

ARCHER

You have told this matter to nobody, brother?

SCRUB

Told! No, sir, I thank you for that; I'm resolved never to   350
speak one word *pro* nor *con*, till we have a peace.

ARCHER

You're i' th' right, brother Scrub. Here's a treaty afoot
between the count and the lady: the priest and the chambermaid are the plenipotentiaries. It shall go hard but I find
a way to be included in the treaty.—Where's the doctor   355
now?

SCRUB

He and Gipsy are this moment devouring my lady's
marmalade in the closet.

AIMWELL (*From without*)

Martin! Martin!

ARCHER

I come, sir, I come.   360

SCRUB

But you forget the other guinea, brother Martin.

ARCHER

Here, I give it with all my heart.

SCRUB

And I take it with all my soul. [*Exit* ARCHER] Ecod, I'll
spoil your plotting, Mrs. Gipsy; and if you should set the
captain upon me, these two guineas will buy me off.   *Exit*   365

Enter MRS. SULLEN *and* DORINDA, *meeting*

MRS. SULLEN

Well, sister!

DORINDA

And well, sister!

MRS. SULLEN

What's become of my lord?

DORINDA

What's become of his servant?

MRS. SULLEN

Servant! He's a prettier fellow, and a finer gentleman by   370
fifty degrees, than his master.

363 s.d. [*Exit* ARCHER] ed. (*Exeunt severally* Q)

DORINDA

O'my conscience, I fancy you could beg that fellow at the gallows-foot!

MRS. SULLEN

O'my conscience, I could, provided I could put a friend of yours in his room.   375

DORINDA

You desired me, sister, to leave you, when you transgressed the bounds of honour.

MRS. SULLEN

Thou dear censorious countrygirl! What dost mean? You can't think of the man without the bedfellow, I find.

DORINDA

I don't find anything unnatural in that thought; while the   380 mind is conversant with flesh and blood, it must conform to the humours of the company.

MRS. SULLEN

How a little love and good company improves a woman! Why, child, you begin to live—you never spoke before.

DORINDA

Because I was never spoke to.—My lord has told me that I   385 have more wit and beauty than any of my sex; and truly I begin to think the man is sincere.

MRS. SULLEN

You're in the right, Dorinda; pride is the life of a woman, and flattery is our daily bread; and she's a fool that won't believe a man there, as much as she that believes him in   390 anything else. But I'll lay you a guinea that I had finer things said to me than you had.

DORINDA

Done! What did your fellow say to ye?

372–5 *beg that fellow at the gallows-foot* . . . Dorinda's point is that Mrs Sullen is so besotted with Archer that she would still be strenuously defending him even if he had been condemned to death on the gallows. Mrs Sullen retaliates by implying that such a fate would be a much more apt ending for Dorinda's gallant, Aimwell. Dorinda is alluding to an ancient custom by which a condemned man's life could be spared, if a woman, petitioning for his reprieve, were prepared to marry him. On several occasions in the eighteenth century, suppliants behaved as if the ancient custom still had some binding force, though their efforts appear to have been uniformly unsuccessful. See Peter Linebaugh, 'The Tyburn Riot against the Surgeons', in Douglas Hay, Peter Linebaugh, John G. Rule, E. P. Thompson, and Cal Winslow, *Albion's Fatal Tree: Crime and Society in Eighteenth-century England* (London, 1975), pp.114–15.

MRS. SULLEN

My fellow took the picture of Venus for mine.

DORINDA

But my lover took me for Venus herself.   395

MRS. SULLEN

Common cant! Had my spark called me a Venus directly,
I should have believed him a footman in good earnest.

DORINDA

But my lover was upon his knees to me.

MRS. SULLEN

And mine was upon his tiptoes to me.

DORINDA

Mine vowed to die for me.   400

MRS. SULLEN

Mine swore to die with me.

DORINDA

Mine spoke the softest moving things.

MRS. SULLEN

Mine had his moving things too.

DORINDA

Mine kissed my hand ten thousand times.

MRS. SULLEN

Mine has all that pleasure to come.   405

DORINDA

Mine offered marriage.

MRS. SULLEN

O Lard! D'ye call that a moving thing?

DORINDA

The sharpest arrow in his quiver, my dear sister! Why, my
ten thousand pounds may lie brooding here this seven
years, and hatch nothing at last but some ill-natured clown   410
like yours. Whereas, if I marry my Lord Aimwell, there will
be title, place, and precedence, the park, the play, and the
drawing-room, splendour, equipage, noise, and flambeaux.—
*Hey, my Lady Aimwell's servants there!—Lights, lights to the
stairs!—My Lady Aimwell's coach put forward!—Stand by,*   415

396 *spark* suitor, lover
401 *to die with me* Mrs Sullen has in mind the very frequent meaning
    of 'die' in seventeenth- and eighteenth-century English—i.e.,
    to reach sexual climax
410 *clown* a country fellow, a rustic; also, an ungenteel or unman-
    nerly person
413 *flambeaux* torches

make room for her ladyship!—Are not these things moving?
What! melancholy of a sudden?

MRS. SULLEN

Happy, happy sister! Your angel has been watchful for your
happiness, whilst mine has slept regardless of his charge.
Long smiling years of circling joys for you, but not one hour   420
for me!   *Weeps*

DORINDA

Come, my dear, we'll talk of something else.

MRS. SULLEN

O Dorinda! I own myself a woman, full of my sex, a gentle,
generous soul, easy and yielding to soft desires; a spacious
heart, where love and all his train might lodge. And must the   425
fair apartment of my breast be made a stable for a brute to
lie in?

DORINDA

Meaning your husband, I suppose?

MRS. SULLEN

Husband! No, even husband is too soft a name for him.—
But come, I expect my brother here tonight or tomorrow; he   430
was abroad when my father married me; perhaps he'll find
a way to make me easy.

DORINDA

Will you promise not to make yourself easy in the meantime
with my lord's friend?

MRS. SULLEN

You mistake me, sister. It happens with us as among the   435
men; the greatest talkers are the greatest cowards: and there's
a reason for it; those spirits evaporate in prattle, which
might do more mischief if they took another course.—
Though, to confess the truth, I do love that fellow;—and if
I met him dressed as he should be, and I undressed as I   440
should be—look ye, sister, I have no supernatural gifts—
I can't swear I could resist the temptation; though I can
safely promise to avoid it; and that's as much as the best of
us can do.   *Exeunt* MRS. SULLEN *and* DORINDA

[Act IV, Scene ii]

[*Scene, the inn*]
Enter AIMWELL *and* ARCHER, *laughing*

ARCHER
And the awkward kindness of the good motherly old
gentlewoman—

AIMWELL
And the coming easiness of the young one.—'Sdeath, 'tis pity
to deceive her!

ARCHER
Nay, if you adhere to those principles, stop where you are.   5

AIMWELL
I can't stop; for I love her to distraction.

ARCHER
'Sdeath, if you love her a hair's breadth beyond discretion, you must go no farther.

AIMWELL
Well, well, anything to deliver us from sauntering away our
idle evenings at White's, Tom's, or Will's, and be stinted to   10
bear looking at our old acquaintance, the cards, because our
impotent pockets can't afford us a guinea for the mercenary
drabs.

ARCHER
Or be obliged to some purse-proud coxcomb for a scandalous
bottle, where we must not pretend to our share of the dis-   15
course, because we can't pay our club o'th' reckoning.—
Damn it, I had rather spunge upon Morris, and sup upon a
dish of bohea scored behind the door!

AIMWELL
And there expose our want of sense by talking criticisms, as
we should our want of money by railing at the government.   20

10 *Tom's* another fashionable London coffee-house
13 *drabs* whores
16 *our club o'th' reckoning* our share of the joint expense
17 *Morris* the owner of a London coffee-house; Farquhar also
mentions him in *Sir Harry Wildair* (V.iv)
18 *bohea* black tea

20 *railing at the government* To many conservative minds, the new-fangled
coffee-houses were places where men idled their time away, 'arraigning
the Judgments and Discretions of their Governors, censuring all their
Actions, and insinuating into the People a Prejudice against them;
extolling and magnifying their own Parts, Knowledge, and Wisdom,

ARCHER

Or be obliged to sneak into the side-box, and between both
houses steal two acts of a play, and because we han't
money to see the other three, we come away discontented and
damn the whole five.

AIMWELL

And ten thousand such rascally tricks—had we outlived our   25
fortunes among our acquaintance.—But now—

ARCHER

Ay, now is the time to prevent all this—strike while the iron
is hot.—This priest is the luckiest part of our adventure;
he shall marry you and pimp for me.

AIMWELL

But I should not like a woman that can be so fond of a   30
Frenchman.

ARCHER

Alas, sir! Necessity has no law. The lady may be in distress;
perhaps she has a confounded husband, and her revenge may
carry her farther than her love. Egad, I have so good an
opinion of her, and of myself, that I begin to fancy strange   35
things; and we must say this for the honour of our women,
and indeed of ourselves, that they do stick to their men, as
they do to their *Magna Carta*. If the plot lies as I suspect, I
must put on the gentleman.—But here comes the doctor—I
shall be ready.   *Exit*   40

Enter FOIGARD

FOIGARD

Sauve you, noble friend.

AIMWELL

O sir, your servant! pray, doctor, may I crave your name?

FOIGARD

Fat naam is upon me? My naam is Foigard, joy.

---

32 *law* liberty or choice (Fitzgibbon)

---

and decrying that of their Rulers; which, if suffered too long, may
prove pernicious and destructive' (*The grand Concern of England ex-
plained* (1673), *The Harleian Miscellany*, vol. 8 (London, 1746), 538).
For some general observations on this attitude, see Robert J. Allen,
The Clubs of Augustan London (Cambridge, Mass., 1933), pp.19–20.

22 *steal two acts* Alluding to the custom that anyone who left the theatre
before the conclusion of the act of the play which was in progress when
he entered should not be charged admission (Hopper and Lahey).

AIMWELL

Foigard! a very good name for a clergyman. Pray, Doctor
Foigard, were you ever in Ireland?   45

FOIGARD

Ireland! no, joy. Fat sort of plaace is dat saam Ireland? Dey
say de people are catched dere when dey are young.

AIMWELL

And some of 'em when they're old—as for example.—(*Takes*
FOIGARD *by the shoulder*) Sir, I arrest you as a traitor against
the government; you're a subject of England, and this   50
morning showed me a commission by which you served as
chaplain in the French army. This is death by our law, and
your reverence must hang for't.

FOIGARD

Upon my shoul, noble friend, dis is strange news you tell me!
Fader Foigard a subject of England! De son of a burgomaster   55
of Brussels, a subject of England! ubooboo—

AIMWELL

The son of a bogtrotter in Ireland! Sir, your tongue will
condemn you before any bench in the kingdom.

FOIGARD

And is my tongue all your evidensh, joy?

AIMWELL

That's enough.   60

FOIGARD

No, no, joy, for I vil never spake English no more.

AIMWELL

Sir, I have other evidence.—Here, Martin! You know this
fellow?

Enter ARCHER

ARCHER (*In a brogue*)

Saave you, my dear cussen, how does your health?

FOIGARD

(*Aside*) Ah! upon my shoul dere is my countryman, and his   65

---

56 *ubooboo* also used by Farquhar as an appropriate exclamation for an
   Irish character in *The Twin Rivals* (V.iii).
57 *bogtrotter* a seventeenth-century nickname for an Irishman—during the
   Exclusion Crisis of Charles II's reign, it had been applied to the
   supporters of the future James II, men of whom Foigard is, in many
   ways, the political heir—see Robert Willman, 'The Origins of "Whig"
   and "Tory" in English Political Language', *The Historical Journal*, vol.
   XVII (1974), 249.

brogue will hang mine.—*Mynheer, Ick wet neat watt hey zacht, Ick universton ewe neat, sacramant.*

AIMWELL

Altering your language won't do, sir; this fellow knows your person, and will swear to your face.

FOIGARD

Faace! Fey, is dear a brogue upon my faash too?   70

ARCHER

Upon my soulvation dere ish, joy!—But cussen Mackshane, vil you not put a remembrance upon me?

FOIGARD (*Aside*)

Mackshane! by St. Paatrick, dat is naame, shure enough.

AIMWELL

I fancy, Archer, you have it.

FOIGARD

The devil hang you, joy! By fat acquaintance are you my   75
cussen?

ARCHER

O, de devil hang yourshelf, joy! You know we were little boys togeder upon de school, and your foster moder's son was married upon my nurse's chister, joy, and so we are Irish cussens.   80

FOIGARD

De devil taak the relation! Vel, joy, and fat school was it?

ARCHER

I tinks is vas—aay—'twas Tipperary.

FOIGARD

No, no, joy; it vas Kilkenny.

AIMWELL

That's enough for us—self-confession. Come, sir, we must deliver you into the hands of the next magistrate.   85

ARCHER

He sends you to gaol, you're tried next assizes, and away you go swing into purgatory.

FOIGARD

And is it so wid you, cussen?

66–7 *Mynheer, Ick wet neat* . . . 'Sir, I don't know what you're saying, I don't understand you, indeed'. Foigard is, of course, attempting to demonstrate, by speaking Flemish, that he is genuinely the son of a burgomaster of Brussels.

82 *Tipperary* a free grammar school, founded in 1669.

83 *Kilkenny* the Protestant college of St John at Kilkenny; Swift and Congreve were among the students educated there.

ARCHER

It vil be sho wid you, cussen, if you don't immediately confess the secret between you and Mrs. Gipsy. Look'ee, sir, the   90
gallows or the secret, take your choice.

FOIGARD

The gallows! Upon my shoul, I hate that saam gallow, for it
is a diseash dat is fatal to our family. Vel, den, dere is
nothing, shentlemens, but Mrs. Shullen would spaak wid the
count in her chamber at midnight, and dere is no haarm,   95
joy, for I am to conduct the count to the plash myshelf.

ARCHER

As I guessed.—Have you communicated the matter to the
count?

FOIGARD

I have not sheen him since.

ARCHER

Right again! Why, then, doctor—you shall conduct me   100
to the lady instead of the count.

FOIGARD

Fat, my cussen to the lady! Upon my shoul, gra, dat is too
much upon the brogue.

ARCHER

Come, come, doctor; consider we have got a rope about your
neck, and if you offer to squeak, we'll stop your windpipe,   105
most certainly: we shall have another job for you in a day
or two, I hope.

AIMWELL

Here's company coming this way; let's into my chamber,
and there concert our affair farther.

ARCHER

Come, my dear cussen, come along.   *Exeunt*   110

Enter BONIFACE, HOUNSLOW, *and* BAGSHOT *at one door,* GIBBET
at the opposite

GIBBET

Well, gentlemen, 'tis a fine night for our enterprise.

HOUNSLOW

Dark as hell.

BAGSHOT

And blows like the devil; our landlord here has showed us
the window where we must break in, and tells us the plate
stands in the wainscot cupboard in the parlour.   115

BONIFACE

Ay, ay, Mr. Bagshot, as the saying is, knives and forks, and

cups and cans, and tumblers and tankards. There's one
tankard, as the saying is, that's near upon as big as me; it
was a present to the squire from his godmother, and smells
of nutmeg and toast like an East India ship.   120

HOUNSLOW

Then you say we must divide at the stairhead?

BONIFACE

Yes, Mr. Hounslow, as the saying is. At one end of that
gallery lies my Lady Bountiful and her daughter, and at the
other Mrs. Sullen. As for the squire—

GIBBET

He's safe enough; I have fairly entered him, and he's more   125
than half-seas-over already. But such a parcel of scoundrels
are got about him now, that, egad, I was ashamed to be
seen in their company.

BONIFACE

'Tis now twelve, as the saying is—gentlemen, you must
set out at one.   130

GIBBET

Hounslow, do you and Bagshot see our arms fixed, and I'll
come to you presently.

HOUNSLOW ⎫
          ⎬ We will.   *Exeunt*
BAGSHOT ⎭

GIBBET

Well, my dear Bonny, you assure me that Scrub is a coward?

BONIFACE

A chicken, as the saying is. You'll have no creature to deal   135
with but the ladies.

GIBBET

And I can assure you, friend, there's a great deal of address
and good manners in robbing a lady; I am the most a
gentleman that way that ever travelled the road.—But, my

117 *cans* small drinking vessels
125 *entered him* started him drinking
126 *half-seas-over* half drunk

138–9 *the most a gentleman* not a completely fanciful touch; one foreign
    visitor to eighteenth-century England was told 'that some highwaymen
    are quite polite and generous, begging to be excused for being forced to
    rob, leaving the passengers the wherewithal to continue their journey'
    (quoted by Asa Briggs (ed.), *How They Lived:* vol. III: *An Anthology
    of original documents written between 1700 and 1815* (Oxford, 1969),
    373–5).

dear Bonny, this prize will be a galleon, a Vigo business. I   140
warrant you we shall bring off three or four thousand
pound.

BONIFACE

In plate, jewels, and money, as the saying is, you may.

GIBBET

Why then, Tyburn, I defy thee! I'll get up to town, sell off
my horse and arms, buy myself some pretty employment   145
in the household, and be as snug and as honest as any
courtier of 'em all.

BONIFACE

And what think you then of my daughter Cherry for a wife?

GIBBET

Look'ee, my dear Bonny—Cherry *is the goddess I adore*, as
the song goes; but it is a maxim that man and wife should   150
never have it in their power to hang one another; for if they
should, the Lord have mercy on 'em both!   *Exeunt*

Act V, [Scene i]

Scene continues: knocking without
Enter BONIFACE

BONIFACE

Coming! coming!—A coach and six foaming horses at this
time o'night! Some great man, as the saying is, for he scorns
to travel with other people.

Enter SIR CHARLES FREEMAN

SIR CHARLES

What, fellow! a public-house, and abed when other people
sleep?   5

BONIFACE

Sir, I an't abed, as the saying is.

---

144 *Tyburn* the usual place of public execution for Middlesex
146 *household* i.e., the royal household; at court
152 s.d. *Exeunt* Q follows this with '*End of the Fourth Act*'

---

140 *Vigo* Sir George Rooke's naval victory on 12 October 1702, at which a
   great deal of valuable booty was taken.
   1 *A coach and six foaming horses* an indication that Sir Charles is a man of
   substantial wealth; cf., for example, the way in which Farquhar's Silvia
   debates her marriage options: 'a moderate fortune, a pretty fellow and a
   pad, or a fine estate, a coach-and-six, and an ass' (*The Recruiting
   Officer*, II.ii).

SIR CHARLES
Is Mr. Sullen's family abed, think'ee?

BONIFACE
All but the squire himself, sir, as the saying is; he's in the house.

SIR CHARLES
What company has he?   10

BONIFACE
Why, sir, there's the constable, Mr. Gauge the exciseman, the hunchbacked barber, and two or three other gentlemen.

SIR CHARLES
I find my sister's letters gave me the true picture of her spouse.

Enter SULLEN, *drunk*

BONIFACE
Sir, here's the squire.   15

SULLEN
The puppies left me asleep.—Sir!

SIR CHARLES
Well, sir.

SULLEN
Sir, I'm an unfortunate man.—I have three thousand pound a year, and I can't get a man to drink a cup of ale with me.   20

SIR CHARLES
That's very hard.

SULLEN
Ay, sir; and unless you have pity upon me, and smoke one pipe with me, I must e'en go home to my wife, and I had rather go [to] the devil by half.

SIR CHARLES
But I presume, sir, you won't see your wife tonight;   25
she'll be gone to bed. You don't use to lie with your wife in that pickle?

SULLEN
What! not lie with my wife! Why, sir, do you take me for an atheist or a rake?

SIR CHARLES
If you hate her, sir, I think you had better lie from her.   30

SULLEN
I think so too, friend. But I'm a justice of peace, and must do nothing against the law.

SIR CHARLES
Law! As I take it, Mr. Justice, nobody observes law for

law's sake, only for the good of those for whom it was made.

SULLEN

But, if the law orders me to send you to gaol, you must lie   35
there, my friend.

SIR CHARLES

Not unless I commit a crime to deserve it.

SULLEN

A crime! 'Oons, an't I married?

SIR CHARLES

Nay, sir, if you call marriage a crime, you must disown it
for a law.   40

SULLEN

Eh! I must be acquainted with you, sir.—But, sir, I should
be very glad to know the truth of this matter.

SIR CHARLES

Truth, sir, is a profound sea, and few there be that dare
wade deep enough to find out the bottom on't. Besides, sir,
I'm afraid the line of your understanding mayn't be long   45
enough.

SULLEN

Look'ee, sir, I have nothing to say to your sea of truth, but,
if a good parcel of land can entitle a man to a little truth, I
have as much as any he in the country.

BONIFACE

I never heard your worship, as the saying is, talk so much   50
before.

SULLEN

Because I never met with a man that I liked before.

BONIFACE

Pray, sir, as the saying is, let me ask you one question: are
not man and wife one flesh?

53–4 *are not man and wife one flesh?* Larson sets against the passage of
dialogue which this question initiates the following passages from
Milton: 'there is no true marriage between them, who agree not in true
consent of mind' (*Prose Works*, III, 290); 'the solace and satisfaction of
the mind is regarded as provided for before the sensitive pleasing of the
body' (ibid., 188); 'This is that rational burning that marriage is to
remedy' (ibid., 192); 'what can be a fouler incongruity, a greater
violence to the reverend secret of nature, than to force a mixture of
minds that cannot unite...?' (ibid., 206); 'Marriage is a human
society . . . if the mind, therefore, cannot have that due company by
marriage that it may reasonably and humanly desire that marriage can
be no human society' (ibid., 210); 'the greatest breach [of mar-
riage] . . . unfitness of mind' (ibid., 210); 'the unity of mind is nearer
and greater than the union of bodies' (ibid., 340).

SIR CHARLES
   You and your wife, Mr. Guts, may be one flesh, because ye   55
   are nothing else; but rational creatures have minds that
   must be united.
SULLEN
   Minds!
SIR CHARLES
   Ay, minds, sir; don't you think that the mind takes place
   of the body?   60
SULLEN
   In some people.
SIR CHARLES
   Then the interest of the master must be consulted before
   that of his servant.
SULLEN
   Sir, you shall dine with me tomorrow!—'Oons, I always
   thought that we were naturally one.   65
SIR CHARLES
   Sir, I know that my two hands are naturally one, because
   they love one another, kiss one another, help one another,
   in all the actions of life; but I could not say so much if they
   were always at cuffs.
SULLEN
   Then 'tis plain that we are two.   70
SIR CHARLES
   Why don't you part with her, sir?
SULLEN
   Will you take her, sir?
SIR CHARLES
   With all my heart.
SULLEN
   You shall have her tomorrow morning, and a venison-pasty
   into the bargain.   75
SIR CHARLES
   You'll let me have her fortune too?
SULLEN
   Fortune! Why, sir, I have no quarrel at her fortune: I only
   hate the woman, sir, and none but the woman shall go.
SIR CHARLES
   But her fortune, sir—
SULLEN
   Can you play at whisk, sir?   80

69 *at cuffs* at blows

SIR CHARLES

No, truly, sir.

SULLEN

Nor at all-fours?

SIR CHARLES

Neither.

SULLEN

(*Aside*) 'Oons! where was this man bred?—Burn me, sir!
I can't go home; 'tis but two a clock.   85

SIR CHARLES

For half an hour, sir, if you please—but you must consider
'tis late.

SULLEN

Late! that's the reason I can't go to bed.—Come, sir! *Exeunt*

Enter CHERRY, *runs across the stage, and knocks at* AIMWELL'*s
chamber-door. Enter* AIMWELL *in his nightcap and gown*

AIMWELL

What's the matter? You tremble, child; you're frighted.

CHERRY

No wonder, sir.—But, in short, sir, this very minute a gang   90
of rogues are gone to rob my Lady Bountiful's house.

AIMWELL

How!

CHERRY

I dogged 'em to the very door, and left 'em breaking in.

AIMWELL

Have you alarmed anybody else with the news?

CHERRY

No, no, sir, I wanted to have discovered the whole plot, and   95
twenty other things, to your man Martin; but I have
searched the whole house and can't find him: where is he?

AIMWELL

No matter, child; will you guide me immediately to the
house?

CHERRY

With all my heart, sir; my Lady Bountiful is my godmother,   100
and I love Mrs. Dorinda so well—

AIMWELL

Dorinda! The name inspires me; the glory and the danger

82 *all-fours* a low game at cards, played by two; so named from the four
   particulars by which it is reckoned, and which, joined in the hands of
   either of the parties, is said to make *all fours*. The *all-four* are *high*, *low*,
   Jack, and the game (Dr Johnson's Dictionary).

shall be all my own.—Come, my life, let me but get my
sword.   *Exeunt*

[Act V, Scene ii]

Scene changes to a bedchamber in LADY BOUNTIFUL'*s house*
Enter MRS. SULLEN, DORINDA, *undressed; a table and lights*

DORINDA
'Tis very late, sister—no news of your spouse yet?
MRS. SULLEN
No, I'm condemned to be alone till towards four, and then
perhaps I may be executed with his company.
DORINDA
Well, my dear, I'll leave you to your rest; you'll go directly
to bed, I suppose.   5
MRS. SULLEN
I don't know what to do.—Heigh-ho!
DORINDA
That's a desiring sigh, sister.
MRS. SULLEN
This is a languishing hour, sister.
DORINDA
And might prove a critical minute if the pretty fellow were
here.   10
MRS. SULLEN
Here! What, in my bedchamber, at two a clock o'th'morning,
I undressed, the family asleep, my hated husband abroad,
and my lovely fellow at my feet!—O gad, sister!
DORINDA
Thoughts are free, sister, and them I allow you.—So, my
dear, good night.   15
MRS. SULLEN
A good rest to my dear Dorinda!—[*Exit* DORINDA] Thoughts
free! Are they so? Why, then, suppose him here, dressed like
a youthful, gay, and burning bridegroom, (*Here* ARCHER
steals out of the closet) with tongue enchanting, eyes be-
witching, knees imploring.—(*Turns a little o' one side, and*   20
sees ARCHER *in the posture she describes*)—Ah!—(*Shrieks, and*
runs to the other side of the stage) Have my thoughts raised a
spirit?—What are you, sir, a man or a devil?
ARCHER
A man, a man, madam.   *Rising*
MRS. SULLEN
How shall I be sure of it?   25

ARCHER

Madam, I'll give you demonstration this minute.

Takes her hand

MRS. SULLEN

What, sir! do you intend to be rude?

ARCHER

Yes, madam, if you please.

MRS. SULLEN

In the name of wonder, whence came ye?

ARCHER

From the skies, madam—I'm a Jupiter in love, and you   30
shall be my Alcmena.

MRS. SULLEN

How came you in?

ARCHER

I flew in at the window, madam; your cousin Cupid lent me
his wings, and your sister Venus opened the casement.

MRS. SULLEN

I'm struck dumb with admiration!   35

ARCHER

And I—with wonder!   *Looks passionately at her*

MRS. SULLEN

What will become of me?

ARCHER

How beautiful she looks!—The teeming jolly spring smiles
in her blooming face, and when she was conceived, her
mother smelt to roses, looked on lilies—   40
     Lilies unfold their white, their fragrant charms,
     When the warm sun thus darts into their arms. *Runs to her*

MRS. SULLEN

Ah!   *Shrieks*

ARCHER

'Oons, madam, what d'ye mean? You'll raise the house.

MRS. SULLEN

Sir, I'll wake the dead before I bear this!—What! approach   45
me with the freedoms of a keeper! I'm glad on't; your
impudence has cured me.

ARCHER

If this be impudence, (*Kneels*) I leave to your partial self;

---

31 *Alcmena* the wife of Amphitryon whom Jupiter seduced by assuming
her husband's appearance. There was a fairly recent, and rather
popular, play on the theme by Dryden—*Amphitryon; or, The Two
Sosias* (first performed in 1690).

no panting pilgrim, after a tedious, painful voyage, e'er
bowed before his saint with more devotion.   50

MRS. SULLEN

(*Aside*) Now, now, I'm ruined, if he kneels!—Rise, thou
prostrate engineer; not all thy undermining skill shall reach
my heart.—Rise, and know, I am a woman without my sex;
I can love to all the tenderness of wishes, sighs, and tears—
but go no farther.—Still, to convince you that I'm more than   55
woman, I can speak my frailty, confess my weakness even for
you—but—

ARCHER

For me!   *Going to lay hold on her*

MRS. SULLEN

Hold, sir, build not upon that; for my most mortal hatred
follows if you disobey what I command you now.—Leave   60
me this minute.—(*Aside*) If he denies, I'm lost.

ARCHER

Then you'll promise—

MRS. SULLEN

Anything another time.

ARCHER

When shall I come?

MRS. SULLEN

Tomorrow—when you will.   65

ARCHER

Your lips must seal the promise.

MRS. SULLEN

Pshaw!

ARCHER

They must! they must! (*Kisses her*)—Raptures and paradise!
—And why not now, my angel? The time, the place, silence,
and secrecy, all conspire. And the now conscious stars have   70
preordained this moment for my happiness.

Takes her in his arms

MRS. SULLEN

You will not! cannot, sure!

ARCHER

If the sun rides fast, and disappoints not mortals of
tomorrow's dawn, this night shall crown my joys.

MRS. SULLEN

My sex's pride assist me!   75

---

52 *engineer* one who designs and constructs military engines for
attack or defence 71 s.d. *in his arms* ed. (*in her arms* Q)

ARCHER
My sex's strength help me!
MRS. SULLEN
You shall kill me first.
ARCHER
I'll die with you.   *Carrying her off*
MRS. SULLEN
Thieves! Thieves! Murder!

Enter SCRUB *in his breeches, and one shoe*

SCRUB
Thieves! Thieves! Murder! Popery!   80
ARCHER
Ha! the very timorous stag will kill in rutting time.
                              Draws and offers to stab SCRUB
SCRUB (*Kneeling*)
O pray, sir, spare all I have, and take my life!
MRS. SULLEN (*Holding* ARCHER'*s hand*)
What does the fellow mean?
SCRUB
O madam, down upon your knees, your marrow-bones!—
he's one of 'em.   85
ARCHER
Of whom?
SCRUB
One of the rogues—I beg your pardon, sir, one of the honest
gentlemen that just now are broke into the house.
ARCHER
How!
MRS. SULLEN
I hope you did not come to rob me?   90
ARCHER
Indeed I did, madam, but I would have taken nothing but
what you might have spared; but your crying 'Thieves' has
waked this dreaming fool, and so he takes 'em for granted.
SCRUB
Granted! 'tis granted, sir; take all we have.
MRS. SULLEN
The fellow looks as if he were broke out of Bedlam.   95
SCRUB
'Oons, madam, they're broke into the house with fire and
sword! I saw them, heard them; they'll be here this minute.

95 *Bedlam* the famous hospital of St Mary of Bethlehem in London,
used as an asylum for the insane

ARCHER
What, thieves!
SCRUB
Under favour, sir, I think so.
MRS. SULLEN
What shall we do, sir?   100
ARCHER
Madam, I wish your ladyship a good night.
MRS. SULLEN
Will you leave me?
ARCHER
Leave you! Lord, madam, did not you command me to be
gone just now, upon pain of your immortal hatred.
MRS. SULLEN
Nay, but pray, sir—   *Takes hold of him*   105
ARCHER
Ha! ha! ha! now comes my turn to be ravished.—You see
now, madam, you must use men one way or other; but take
this by the way, good madam, that none but a fool will give
you the benefit of his courage, unless you'll take his love
along with it.—How are they armed, friend?   110
SCRUB
With sword and pistol, sir.
ARCHER
Hush!—I see a dark lanthorn coming through the gallery.—
Madam, be assured I will protect you, or lose my life.
MRS. SULLEN
Your life! No, sir, they can rob me of nothing that I value
half so much; therefore, now, sir, let me entreat you to be   115
gone.
ARCHER
No, madam, I'll consult my own safety for the sake of yours;
I'll work by stratagem. Have you courage enough to stand
the appearance of 'em?
MRS. SULLEN
Yes, yes, since I have scaped your hands, I can face anything. 120
ARCHER
Come hither, brother Scrub! Don't you know me?

112 *dark lanthorn* a lantern with an arrangement by which the light
     can be concealed
118 *stratagem* 'a politick Device, or subtil Invention in War' (Nathan
     Bailey, *An Universal Etymological English Dictionary* (London,
     1721))

SCRUB

Eh, my dear brother, let me kiss thee!   *Kisses* ARCHER

ARCHER

This way—here—   ARCHER *and* SCRUB *hide behind the bed*

Enter GIBBET *with a dark lanthorn in one hand and a pistol in t'other*

GIBBET

Ay, ay, this is the chamber, and the lady alone.

MRS. SULLEN

Who are you, sir? What would you have? D'ye come to rob   125
me?

GIBBET

Rob you! Alack a day, madam, I'm only a younger brother,
madam; and so, madam, if you make a noise, I'll shoot you
through the head; but don't be afraid, madam.—(*Laying his
lanthorn and pistol upon the table*) These rings, madam;   130
don't be concerned, madam, I have a profound respect for
you, madam; your keys, madam; don't be frighted, madam,
I'm the most of a gentleman.—(*Searching her pockets*)
This necklace, madam; I never was rude to a lady;—I have
a veneration—for this necklace—   135

Here ARCHER, *having come round and seized the pistol, takes*
GIBBET *by the collar, trips up his heels, and claps the pistol*
to his breast

ARCHER

Hold, profane villain, and take the reward of thy sacrilege!

GIBBET

O! pray, sir, don't kill me; I an't prepared.

ARCHER

How many is there of 'em, Scrub?

SCRUB

Five and forty, sir.

ARCHER

Then I must kill the villain, to have him out of the way.   140

GIBBET

Hold, hold, sir, we are but three, upon my honour.

ARCHER

Scrub, will you undertake to secure him?

SCRUB

Not I, sir; kill him, kill him!

ARCHER

Run to Gipsy's chamber, there you'll find the doctor; bring

135 s.d. *pistol* ed. (*Pistols* Q)

him hither presently.—(*Exit* SCRUB, *running*) Come, rogue, if   145
you have a short prayer, say it.
GIBBET
Sir, I have no prayer at all; the government has provided a
chaplain to say prayers for us on these occasions.
MRS. SULLEN
Pray, sir, don't kill him: you fright me as much as him.
ARCHER
The dog shall die, madam, for being the occasion of my dis-   150
appointment.—Sirrah, this moment is your last.
GIBBET
Sir, I'll give you two hundred pound to spare my life.
ARCHER
Have you no more, rascal?
GIBBET
Yes, sir, I can command four hundred; but I must reserve
two of 'em to save my life at the sessions.   155

Enter SCRUB *and* FOIGARD

ARCHER
Here, doctor, I suppose Scrub and you between you may
manage him. Lay hold of him, doctor.
                                      FOIGARD *lays hold of* GIBBET
GIBBET
What! turned over to the priest already!—Look ye, doctor,
you come before your time; I an't condemned yet, I thank ye.
FOIGARD
Come, my dear joy, I vil secure your body and your shoul   160
too; I vil make you a good Catholic, and give you an
absolution.
GIBBET
Absolution! Can you procure me a pardon, doctor?
FOIGARD
No, joy.

---

145 *presently* immediately

147–8 *the government has provided a chaplain* '. . . a Divine is allwayes
appointed to be with them in the prison to prepare them for their death
by makeing them sencible of their crimes and all their sins, and to
confess and repent of them; these do accompany them to the place of
execution . . . there after they have prayed and spoken to the people the
Minister does exhort them to repent and to forgive all the world'
(Christopher Morris (ed.), *The Journeys of Celia Fiennes* (London,
1949), p.310).

GIBBET

Then you and your absolution may go to the devil!   165

ARCHER

Convey him into the cellar, there bind him:—take the pistol, and if he offers to resist, shoot him through the head—and come back to us with all the speed you can.

SCRUB

Ay, ay, come, doctor, do you hold him fast, and I'll guard him.   170

[Exeunt FOIGARD *and* GIBBET, SCRUB *following]*

MRS. SULLEN

But how came the doctor—

ARCHER

In short, madam—(*Shrieking without*) 'Sdeath! the rogues are at work with the other ladies—I'm vexed I parted with the pistol; but I must fly to their assistance.—Will you stay here, madam, or venture yourself with me?   175

MRS. SULLEN

O, with you, dear sir, with you.

Takes him by the arm and exeunt

[Act V, Scene iii]

Scene changes to another apartment in the same house
Enter HOUNSLOW *dragging in* LADY BOUNTIFUL, *and* BAGSHOT
hauling in DORINDA; *the rogues with swords drawn*

HOUNSLOW

Come, come, your jewels, mistress!

BAGSHOT

Your keys, your keys, old gentlewoman!

Enter AIMWELL *and* CHERRY

AIMWELL

Turn this way, villains! I durst engage an army in such a cause.   *He engages 'em both*

DORINDA

O madam, had I but a sword to help the brave man!   5

LADY BOUNTIFUL

There's three or four hanging up in the hall; but they won't draw. I'll go fetch one, however.   *Exit*

Enter ARCHER *and* MRS. SULLEN

s.d. *Enter* HOUNSLOW . . . As Strauss pointed out, the stage directions suggest that 'the speeches of the two robbers should be interchanged'.

ARCHER

Hold, hold, my lord! every man his bird, pray.

They engage man to man; the rogues are thrown and disarmed

CHERRY (*Aside*)

What! the rogues taken! then they'll impeach my father:
I must give him timely notice.   *Runs out*   10

ARCHER

Shall we kill the rogues?

AIMWELL

No, no, we'll bind them.

ARCHER

Ay, ay.—(*To* MRS. SULLEN, *who stands by him*) Here, madam,
lend me your garter.

MRS. SULLEN

(*Aside*) The devil's in this fellow! He fights, loves, and   15
banters, all in a breath.—Here's a cord that the rogues
brought with 'em, I suppose.

ARCHER

Right, right, the rogue's destiny, a rope to hang himself.—
Come, my lord—this is but a scandalous sort of an office
(*Binding the rogues together*), if our adventures should end in   20
this sort of hangman-work; but I hope there is something
in prospect that—

Enter SCRUB

Well, Scrub, have you secured your Tartar?

SCRUB

Yes, sir, I left the priest and him disputing about religion.

AIMWELL

And pray carry these gentlemen to reap the benefit of the   25
controversy.

Delivers the prisoners to SCRUB, **who leads 'em out**

MRS. SULLEN

Pray, sister, how came my lord here?

DORINDA

And pray, how came the gentleman here?

MRS. SULLEN

I'll tell you the greatest piece of villainy—

They talk in dumb show

AIMWELL

I fancy, Archer, you have been more successful in your   30
adventures than the housebreakers.

23 *Tartar* a man of savage disposition; but, also, a thief

ARCHER

No matter for my adventure, yours is the principal.—Press
her this minute to marry you—now while she's hurried
between the palpitation of her fear and the joy of her
deliverance, now while the tide of her spirits are at high-   35
flood—throw yourself at her feet, speak some romantic
nonsense or other—address her like Alexander in the
height of his victory, confound her senses, bear down her
reason, and away with her.—The priest is now in the
cellar, and dare not refuse to do the work.   40

Enter LADY BOUNTIFUL

AIMWELL

But how shall I get off without being observed?

ARCHER

You a lover, and not find a way to get off!—Let me see—

AIMWELL

You bleed, Archer.

ARCHER

'Sdeath, I'm glad on't; this wound will do the business. I'll
amuse the old lady and Mrs. Sullen about dressing my   45
wound, while you carry off Dorinda.

LADY BOUNTIFUL

Gentlemen, could we understand how you would be gratified
for the services—

ARCHER

Come, come, my lady, this is no time for compliments; I'm
wounded, madam.   50

LADY BOUNTIFUL ⎫
MRS. SULLEN ⎬ How! wounded!
          ⎭

DORINDA

I hope, sir, you have received no hurt?

AIMWELL

None but what you may cure—   *Makes love in dumb show*

LADY BOUNTIFUL

Let me see your arm, sir—I must have some powder-
sugar to stop the blood.—O me! an ugly gash upon my word,   55
sir: you must go into bed.

ARCHER

Ay, my lady, a bed would do very well.—(*To* MRS. SULLEN)
Madam, will you do me the favour to conduct me to a
chamber?

LADY BOUNTIFUL

Do, do, daughter—while I get the lint and the probe and the 60
plaister ready.

Runs out one way, AIMWELL *carries off* DORINDA *another*

ARCHER

Come, madam, why don't you obey your mother's
commands?

MRS. SULLEN

How can you, after what is past, have the confidence to ask
me? 65

ARCHER

And if you go to that, how can you, after what is past, have the
confidence to deny me? Was not this blood shed in your
defence, and my life exposed for your protection? Look ye,
madam, I'm none of your romantic fools, that fight giants
and monsters for nothing; my valour is downright Swiss; 70
I'm a soldier of fortune, and must be paid.

MRS. SULLEN

'Tis ungenerous in you, sir, to upbraid me with your
services.

ARCHER

'Tis ungenerous in you, madam, not to reward 'em.

MRS. SULLEN

How! At the expense of my honour? 75

ARCHER

Honour! Can honour consist with ingratitude? If you would
deal like a woman of honour, do like a man of honour. D'ye
think I would deny you in such a case?

Enter a SERVANT

SERVANT

Madam, my lady ordered me to tell you that your brother is
below at the gate. 80

MRS. SULLEN

My brother! Heavens be praised!—Sir, he shall thank you
for your services; he has it in his power.

ARCHER

Who is your brother, madam?

---

60 *probe* a surgical instrument for exploring wounds

---

70 *Swiss* i.e., a mercenary—among other activities, Swiss mercenary soldiers provided a special bodyguard for the French kings.

MRS. SULLEN

Sir Charles Freeman.—You'll excuse me, sir; I must go and
receive him.   [*Exit*]   85

ARCHER

Sir Charles Freeman! 'Sdeath and hell! my old acquaintance.
Now unless Aimwell has made good use of his time, all our
fair machine goes souse into the sea like the Eddystone.

Exit

[Act V, Scene iv]

Scene changes to the gallery in the same house
Enter AIMWELL *and* DORINDA

DORINDA

Well, well, my lord, you have conquered; your late generous
action will, I hope, plead for my easy yielding, though I
must own your lordship had a friend in the fort before.

AIMWELL

The sweets of Hybla dwell upon her tongue!—Here,
doctor—   5

Enter FOIGARD *with a book*

FOIGARD

Are you prepared boat?

DORINDA

I'm ready. But first, my lord, one word.—I have a frightful
example of a hasty marriage in my own family; when I reflect
upon't it shocks me. Pray, my lord, consider a little—

AIMWELL

Consider! Do you doubt my honour or my love?   10

DORINDA

Neither; I do believe you equally just as brave: and were
your whole sex drawn out for me to choose, I should not
cast a look upon the multitude if you were absent. But, my
lord, I'm a woman; colours, concealments may hide a
thousand faults in me. Therefore know me better first; I   15
hardly dare affirm I know myself in anything except my
love.

88 *machine* a military engine, siege-tower, or the like
4 *Hybla* a town in Sicily, famous for its honey

88 *Eddystone* The first Eddystone lighthouse, completed in 1699, was
destroyed in the great storm of 27 November 1703.

AIMWELL

(*Aside*) Such goodness who could injure! I find myself un-
equal to the task of villain; she has gained my soul, and
made it honest like her own. I cannot, cannot hurt her.—   20
Doctor, retire.—(*Exit* FOIGARD) Madam, behold your lover
and your proselyte, and judge of my passion by my conver-
sion!—I'm all a lie, nor dare I give a fiction to your arms;
I'm all counterfeit, except my passion.

DORINDA

Forbid it, Heaven! A counterfeit!   25

AIMWELL

I am no lord, but a poor, needy man, come with a mean, a
scandalous design to prey upon your fortune; but the
beauties of your mind and person have so won me from
myself that, like a trusty servant, I prefer the interest of my
mistress to my own.   30

DORINDA

Sure I have had the dream of some poor mariner, a sleepy
image of a welcome port, and wake involved in storms!—
Pray, sir, who are you?

AIMWELL

Brother to the man whose title I usurped, but stranger to
his honour or his fortune.   35

DORINDA

Matchless honesty!—Once I was proud, sir, of your
wealth and title, but now am prouder that you want it: now
I can show my love was justly levelled, and had no aim but
love.—Doctor, come in.

Enter FOIGARD *at one door*, GIPSY *at another, who whispers*
DORINDA

[*To* FOIGARD] Your pardon, sir, we shan't want you now.—   40
[*To* AIMWELL] Sir, you must excuse me—I'll wait on you
presently.   *Exit with* GIPSY

FOIGARD

Upon my shoul, now, dis is foolish.   *Exit*

AIMWELL

Gone! And bid the priest depart!—It has an ominous look.

Enter ARCHER

ARCHER

Courage, Tom!—Shall I wish you joy?   45

40 *we shan't want you now* ed. (we shannot; won't you now Q)

AIMWELL

No.

ARCHER

'Oons, man, what ha' you been doing?

AIMWELL

O Archer! My honesty, I fear, has ruined me.

ARCHER

How?

AIMWELL

I have discovered myself.   50

ARCHER

Discovered! and without my consent? What! have I embarked my small remains in the same bottom with yours,
and you dispose of all without my partnership?

AIMWELL

O Archer! I own my fault.

ARCHER

After conviction—'tis then too late for pardon.—You may   55
remember, Mr. Aimwell, that you proposed this folly: as
you begun, so end it. Henceforth I'll hunt my fortune single
—so farewell!

AIMWELL

Stay, my dear Archer, but a minute.

ARCHER

Stay! What, to be despised, exposed, and laughed at! No, I   60
would sooner change conditions with the worst of the rogues
we just now bound than bear one scornful smile from the
proud knight that once I treated as my equal.

AIMWELL

What knight?

ARCHER

Sir Charles Freeman, brother to the lady that I had almost   65
—but no matter for that, 'tis a cursed night's work, and so I
leave you to make your best on't.   *Going*

AIMWELL

Freeman!—One word, Archer. Still I have hopes; methought she received my confession with pleasure.

ARCHER

'Sdeath! who doubts it?   70

AIMWELL

She consented after to the match; and still I dare believe
she will be just.

ARCHER

To herself, I warrant her, as you should have been.

AIMWELL
By all my hopes, she comes, and smiling comes.

Enter DORINDA, *mighty gay*

DORINDA
Come, my dear lord—I fly with impatience to your arms—   75
the minutes of my absence was a tedious year. Where's this
tedious priest?

Enter FOIGARD

ARCHER
'Oons, a brave girl!

DORINDA
I suppose, my lord, this gentleman is privy to our affairs?

ARCHER
Yes, yes, madam, I'm to be your father.   80

DORINDA
Come, priest, do your office.

ARCHER
Make haste, make haste, couple 'em any way. (*Takes*
AIMWELL'*s hand*) Come, madam, I'm to give you—

DORINDA
My mind's altered; I won't.

ARCHER
Eh!   85

AIMWELL
I'm confounded!

FOIGARD
Upon my shoul, and sho is myshelf.

ARCHER
What's the matter now, madam?

DORINDA
Look ye, sir, one generous action deserves another. This
gentleman's honour obliged him to hide nothing from me;   90
my justice engages me to conceal nothing from him. In short,
sir, you are the person that you thought you counterfeited;
you are the true Lord Viscount Aimwell, and I wish your
lordship joy.—Now, priest, you may be gone; if my lord is
pleased now with the match, let his lordship marry me in the   95
face of the world.

AIMWELL ⎫
            ⎬ What does she mean?
ARCHER ⎭

76–7 *tedious* the awkward repetition of 'tedious' here may be a printing
error.

DORINDA
Here's a witness for my truth.

Enter SIR CHARLES [FREEMAN] *and* MRS. SULLEN

SIR CHARLES
My dear Lord Aimwell, I wish you joy.
AIMWELL
Of what?   100
SIR CHARLES
Of your honour and estate. Your brother died the day before
I left London; and all your friends have writ after you to
Brussels—among the rest I did myself the honour.
ARCHER
Hark ye, sir knight, don't you banter now?
SIR CHARLES
'Tis truth, upon my honour.   105
AIMWELL
Thanks to the pregnant stars that formed this accident!
ARCHER
Thanks to the womb of time that brought it forth!—away
with it!
AIMWELL
Thanks to my guardian angel that led me to the prize!
                                         Taking DORINDA'*s hand*
ARCHER
And double thanks to the noble Sir Charles Freeman.—My   110
lord, I wish you joy. My lady, I wish you joy.—Egad, Sir
Freeman, you're the honestest fellow living.—'Sdeath, I'm
grown strange airy upon this matter!—My lord, how d'ye?—
A word, my lord; don't you remember something of a
previous agreement, that entitles me to the moiety of this   115
lady's fortune, which, I think, will amount to five thousand
pound?
AIMWELL
Not a penny, Archer; you would ha' cut my throat just now,
because I would not deceive this lady.
ARCHER
Ay, and I'll cut your throat again, if you should deceive her 120
now.
AIMWELL
That's what I expected; and to end the dispute, the lady's

113 *airy* full of life and high spirits
115 *moiety* half

fortune is ten thousand pound, we'll divide stakes: take the
ten thousand pound or the lady.

DORINDA

How! is your lordship so indifferent?   125

ARCHER

No, no, no, madam! his lordship knows very well that I'll
take the money; I leave you to his lordship, and so we're
both provided for.

Enter COUNT BELLAIR

COUNT BELLAIR

Mesdames et Messieurs, I am your servant trice humble! I
hear you be rob here.   130

AIMWELL

The ladies have been in some danger, sir.

COUNT BELLAIR

And, begar, our inn be rob too!

AIMWELL

Our inn! By whom?

COUNT BELLAIR

By the landlord, begar!—Garzoon, he has rob himself and
run away!   135

ARCHER

Robbed himself!

COUNT BELLAIR

Ay, begar, and me too of a hundre pound.

ARCHER

A hundred pound?

COUNT BELLAIR

Yes, that I owed him.

AIMWELL

Our money's gone, Frank.   140

ARCHER

Rot the money! my wench is gone.—*Savez-vous quelquechose
de Mademoiselle Cherry?*

Enter a FELLOW *with a strongbox and a letter*

FELLOW

Is there one Martin here?

ARCHER

Ay, ay—who wants him?

141–2 *Savez-vous quelquechose de Mademoiselle Cherry?* Do you know
    anything about Miss Cherry?

FELLOW

I have a box here, and letter for him.   145

ARCHER

(*Taking the box*) Ha! ha! ha! what's here? Legerdemain!—
By this light, my lord, our money again!—But this unfolds
the riddle.—(*Opening the letter, reads*) Hum, hum, hum—O,
'tis for the public good and must be communicated to the
company.   [*Reads*]   150

Mr. Martin,

*My father, being afraid of an impeachment by the rogues that
are taken tonight, is gone off; but, if you can procure him a
pardon, he will make great discoveries that may be useful to the
country. Could I have met you instead of your master tonight, I*   155
*would have delivered myself into your hands with a sum that
much exceeds that in your strongbox, which I have sent you,
with an assurance to my dear Martin, that I shall ever be his
most faithful friend till death.*

CHERRY BONIFACE   160

There's a billet-doux for you! As for the father, I think he
ought to be encouraged; and for the daughter—pray, my
lord, persuade your bride to take her into her service instead
of Gipsy.

AIMWELL

I can assure you, madam, your deliverance was owing to her   165
discovery.

DORINDA

Your command, my lord, will do without the obligation. I'll
take care of her.

SIR CHARLES

This good company meets opportunely in favour of a design
I have in behalf of my unfortunate sister. I intend to part   170
her from her husband—gentlemen, will you assist me?

ARCHER

Assist you! 'Sdeath, who would not?

COUNT BELLAIR

Assist! Garzoon, we all assest!

Enter SULLEN

SULLEN

What's all this? They tell me, spouse, that you had like to
have been robbed.   175

161 *billet-doux* love letter

MRS. SULLEN

Truly, spouse, I was pretty near it, had not these two gentlemen interposed.

SULLEN

How came these gentlemen here?

MRS. SULLEN

That's his way of returning thanks, you must know.

COUNT BELLAIR

Garzoon, the question be apropos for all dat.   180

SIR CHARLES

You promised last night, sir, that you would deliver your lady
to me this morning.

SULLEN

Humph!

ARCHER

Humph! What do you mean by humph? Sir, you shall deliver
her—in short, sir, we have saved you and your family; and   185
if you are not civil, we'll unbind the rogues, join with 'em,
and set fire to your house. What does the man mean? Not
part with his wife!

COUNT BELLAIR

Ay, garzoon, de man no understan common justice.

MRS. SULLEN

Hold, gentlemen, all things here must move by consent; com-   190
pulsion would spoil us. Let my dear and I talk the matter
over, and you shall judge it between us.

SULLEN

Let me know first who are to be our judges.—Pray, sir, who
are you?

SIR CHARLES

I am Sir Charles Freeman, come to take away your wife.   195

SULLEN

And you, good sir?

AIMWELL

Charles Viscount Aimwell, come to take away your sister.

SULLEN

And you, pray, sir?

ARCHER

Francis Archer, Esq., come—

SULLEN

To take away my mother, I hope. Gentlemen, you're heartily   200
welcome; I never met with three more obliging people since

197 *Charles Viscount Aimwell* He has previously been called Tom.

I was born!—And now, my dear, if you please, you shall have
the first word.

ARCHER

And the last, for five pound!

MRS. SULLEN

Spouse!   205

SULLEN

Rib!

MRS. SULLEN

How long have we been married?

SULLEN

By the almanac, fourteen months; but by my account, fourteen
years.

MRS. SULLEN

'Tis thereabout by my reckoning.   210

COUNT BELLAIR

Garzoon, their account will agree.

MRS. SULLEN

Pray, spouse, what did you marry for?

SULLEN

To get an heir to my estate.

SIR CHARLES

And have you succeeded?

SULLEN

No.   215

ARCHER

The condition fails of his side.—Pray, madam, what did you
marry for?

MRS. SULLEN

To support the weakness of my sex by the strength of his, and
to enjoy the pleasures of an agreeable society.

SIR CHARLES

Are your expectations answered?   220

MRS. SULLEN

No.

COUNT BELLAIR

A clear case! a clear case!

---

206 *Rib* an allusion, of course, to the creation of Eve from one of Adam's
ribs (Genesis 2: 21, 22), and an attempt by Sullen to emphasize a
husband's authority over his wife. The fact that Eve had been created
from a rib rather than, for example, from some part of the head was
conventionally interpreted as signifying the man's superiority to the
woman—a superiority Mrs Sullen later implicitly acknowledges by her
reference to 'the weakness of my sex' (V.iv, 218).

SIR CHARLES
What are the bars to your mutual contentment?
MRS. SULLEN
In the first place, I can't drink ale with him.
SULLEN
Nor can I drink tea with her. 225
MRS. SULLEN
I can't hunt with you.
SULLEN
Nor can I dance with you.
MRS. SULLEN
I hate cocking and racing.
SULLEN
And I abhor ombre and piquet.
MRS. SULLEN
Your silence is intolerable. 230
SULLEN
Your prating is worse.
MRS. SULLEN
Have we not been a perpetual offence to each other? a
gnawing vulture at the heart?
SULLEN
A frightful goblin to the sight?
MRS. SULLEN
A porcupine to the feeling? 235
SULLEN
Perpetual wormwood to the taste?
MRS. SULLEN
Is there on earth a thing we could agree in?
SULLEN
Yes—to part.
MRS. SULLEN
With all my heart.
SULLEN
Your hand. 240
MRS. SULLEN
Here.
SULLEN
These hands joined us, these shall part us.—Away!

228 *cocking* cock-fighting
229 *ombre* a very popular card game of the period, played by three
persons with forty cards
229 *piquet* a card game played by two persons with a pack of
thirty-two cards

MRS. SULLEN
  North.
SULLEN
  South.
MRS. SULLEN
  East.   245
SULLEN
  West—far as the poles asunder.
COUNT BELLAIR
  Begar, the ceremony be vera pretty!
SIR CHARLES
  Now, Mr. Sullen, there wants only my sister's fortune to
  make us easy.
SULLEN
  Sir Charles, you love your sister, and I love her fortune;   250
  every one to his fancy.
ARCHER
  Then you won't refund?
SULLEN
  Not a stiver.
ARCHER
  Then I find, madam, you must e'en go to your prison again.
COUNT BELLAIR
  What is the portion?   255
SIR CHARLES
  Ten thousand pound, sir.
COUNT BELLAIR
  Garzoon, I'll pay it, and she shall go home wid me.
ARCHER
  Ha! ha! ha! French all over.—Do you know, sir, what ten
  thousand pound English is?
COUNT BELLAIR
  No, begar, not justement.   260
ARCHER
  Why, sir, 'tis a hundred thousand livres.
COUNT BELLAIR
  A hundre tousand livres! Ah! garzoon, me canno' do't, your
  beauties and their fortunes are both too much for me.
ARCHER
  Then I will.—This night's adventure has proved strangely
  lucky to us all—for Captain Gibbet in his walk had made   265

253 *stiver* a Dutch coin of very small value
261 *livres* an old French money of account divided into twenty sous

bold, Mr. Sullen, with your study and escritoire, and had
taken out all the writings of your estate, all the articles of
marriage with his lady, bills, bonds, leases, receipts to an
infinite value: I took 'em from him, and I deliver them to Sir
Charles.   *Gives him a parcel of papers and parchments*   270

SULLEN

How, my writings!—my head aches consumedly.—Well,
gentlemen, you shall have her fortune, but I can't talk. If you
have a mind, Sir Charles, to be merry, and celebrate my
sister's wedding and my divorce, you may command my
house—but my head aches consumedly.—Scrub, bring me   275
a dram.

ARCHER

(*To* MRS. SULLEN) Madam, there's a country dance to the
trifle that I sung today; your hand, and we'll lead it up.
                                                            Here a dance
'Twould be hard to guess which of these parties is the better
pleased, the couple joined, or the couple parted; the one   280
rejoicing in hopes of an untasted happiness, and the other
in their deliverance from an experienced misery.

> Both happy in their several states we find,
> Those parted by consent, and those conjoined.
> Consent, if mutual, saves the lawyer's fee.   285
> Consent is law enough to set you free.

266 *escritoire* writing-desk
286 *set you free* Q follows this with '*FINIS*'

AN EPILOGUE
Designed to be spoke in The Beaux' Stratagem

If to our play your judgment can't be kind,
Let its expiring author pity find:
Survey his mournful case with melting eyes,
Nor let the bard be damned before he dies.
Forbear, you fair, on his last scene to frown,   5
But his true exit with a plaudit crown;
Then shall the dying poet cease to fear
The dreadful knell, while your applause he hears.
At Leuctra so the conquering Theban died,
Claimed his friends' praises, but their tears denied: 10
Pleased in the pangs of death, he greatly thought
Conquest with loss of life but cheaply bought.
The difference this, the Greek was one would fight,
As brave, though not so gay, as Sergeant Kite;
Ye sons of Will's, what's that to those who write?   15
To Thebes alone, the Grecian owed his bays; ⎫
You may the bard above the hero raise,   ⎬
Since yours is greater than Athenian praise. ⎭

14 *Kite* one of the main characters in Farquhar's preceding comedy,
The Recruiting Officer
16 *bays* a triumphal wreath for a conqueror or for a poet

EPILOGUE In the 1736 collected edition of Farquhar's works, the
epilogue is said to be 'By Mr. SMITH, the Author of PHAEDRA AND
HYPOLITUS'. It is difficult to know how much trust to put in this
identification, but Edmund Smith (1672–1710) is, in fact, a not unlikely
candidate for this particular role. As a result of numerous indiscretions,
he had been expelled from Oxford in December 1705 and was thus
compelled to earn his living by his pen. His dramatic retelling of the
Phaedra story was one of the most ambitious of his attempts to
establish himself on the London literary scene; it received its first
performance on 21 April 1707—about six weeks, that is, after the first
performance of *The Beaux' Stratagem*—and was staged by the same
company as had given the premiere of Farquhar's play. Thus, as far as
the possibility of his having composed this epilogue is concerned, he
was definitely in the right place at the right time.
2 *expiring author* Farquhar was, of course, mortally ill during the writing
of *The Beaux' Stratagem* and died only a few weeks after its first
performance.
9 *Leuctra* At the battle of Leuctra, 371 B.C., the Thebans, led by
Epaminondas, defeated the Spartans. However, the Theban general did
not, in fact, die in the moment of his victory.